Fin Treasure

Using ancient and modern devices

in New England

by Theodore Parker Burbank

For additional copies or more information, please contact:

Salty Pilgrim Press
17 Causeway Street
Millis, MA 02054 USA
1 508 794-1200
captain@saltypilgrim.com

First Edition

ISBN 978-1-935616-15-3

Copyright © 2016 by Theodore P Burbank

Printed in the USA

Forward

Two Keys to Success Finding Treasure

There are two foundational things you must have and do in order to attain success in treasure hunting: research and proper tools. This book addresses both in depth.

1) Research

Research, quality research, is of paramount importance in successfully locating and retrieving treasure and other valuables.

We have chronicled hundreds, if not thousands, of places where you can find your treasure trove. Places where others have found some and where perhaps you, using the unique methods this book reveals, will find more.

Four categories of likely sources of treasure which we have researched for you are:

Shipwrecks

Shipwrecks along the outer Cape and the rocky coast of Maine are what legends are made of. Thousands of ships, and their crews, have met their end on the shifting sands of Cape Cod, for centuries known as the "Graveyard of The Atlantic." The icy cold waters of the rocky coast of Maine have claimed its share of hapless ships and seamen as well.

Each of these ships and every one of the mariners carried valuables, and in the case of pirates; gold, silver, jewelry, diamonds, rubies etc. These treasures are perhaps the most difficult to recover however, it might be argued, the most rewarding.

A perfect example of this is the locating of the pirate ship Whydah that went down off Cape Cod in an April storm in 1779. Millions have been recovered and million more await salvaging. You might want to visit the wonderful Whydah Pirate Museum on route 28 in Yarmouth or Expebition Whydah on Macmillan Pier across from the ferry terminal in Provincetown, both on Cape Cod.

We are not suggesting you learn to scuba dive to find shipwreck treasures, although of course you can. Rather, while walking on a beach many have found a gold coin or other ancient or modern valuables, without even looking.

Pirate Treasure

The words pirates and New England are seldom found in the same sentence. One generally associates the Caribbean and other warmer climes with pirates. One usually can't imagine pirates wearing earmuffs and heavy jackets for protection against harsh New England winter weather. Yet New England, especially Newport, Rhodes Island, was the pirate capital of the world in the late 1700s and the early 1800s.

Therefore, many pirates, famous and not so famous, have plied the coast of New England for centuries. Who were the pirates of New England? Why were they here? Where might they have left treasure behind and why would they sail away without it? Tales of where the pirates have and may have buried and hidden their loot along with places where some of it has been found, are told in these pages. Has all the treasure been found? Might you find the largest cache of all?

With the help of the tips in this book you very well might.

Hidden Treasures

Gold, Silver, Coins and Jewels were not only buried/hidden by pirates but were hidden by merchant, farmers and regular folk alike all over New England. You might ask why? The answer: banks and other institutions were either; not available in rural places or too far away to conveniently reach by horse and buggy. Perhaps the biggest reason was that many, if not most people in the 18ᵗʰ and 19ᵗʰ centuries did not trust banks.

As a result, many times a person who had secreted their fortune in the cellar of their home's foundation or in a can buried in the yard, died before telling anyone where their fortune lay.

Hints and suggestions on finding abandoned homes as well as entire abandoned towns are included here.

Nature's Treasures

There's gold in them thar streams and hills! Yes, gold, silver and valuable gems can be found in some of New England's many streams, hills, mountains and other locations. You may be surprised how accessible these valuable deposits are. We list the places where you might begin your search and find your own treasure.

You don't have to travel to Colorado to pan for gold or explore the site of an abandoned goldmine when you can have success and fun doing it right here in New England.

2) Proper Tools

"The right tools can make anyone an expert." This old adage is no more true than when applied to treasure hunting.

a) We go into great depth explaining how to use *Time Tested Treasure Hunting Tools.* These tools have been used for centuries; tools that you can buy or make on your own.

Imagine what you might find if you had a simple, low cost or free tool(s), no batteries required, that could point you to such treasures! These century-tested devices are revealed in this book.

b) Modern metal detecting equipment come in many configurations and prices and can add greatly to your success and pleasure hunting for treasure.

Table of Contents

The Ancient
Art of
Dowsing
Made Easy

Tools and Tips for Finding Treasure

We will be listing tools, some ancient, some modern you can use in finding treasures and much more. The ancient tools have been employed in finding/locating: Sunken or Buried Treasure, and much more.

Ancient Tools – Dowsing

Dowsing is not only used to find water. Amazingly, dowsing has been employed for centuries in locating; buried and sunken treasures, gold, silver, buried foundations, archaeological sites, gems, coal, oil, underground pipes and electrical lines, lost children and pets, murderers, thieves, liars and much more. Essentially, dowsing can be used to determine and/or find whatever one wants.

What is Dowsing?

Dowsing a/k/a Water Witching, Divining, Questing and Doodlebuging is the ancient art of finding water, minerals and other objects using various dowsing devices. Exactly how it works is controversial. Many theorize that objects have a natural magnetic, electromagnetic or other perhaps unknown energies that are detected and demonstrated via the dowsing device.

Many feel that dowsing abilities should be considered no more mysterious than seeing, hearing or feeling, and appear to be natural to all of us. Dowsing skills improve quickly with practice.

A Bit of History

Dowsing with: L-rods, forked branches, pendulums, bobbers, and other devices dates back to the era BC and even before recorded history.

Examples:
- A cave drawing of a dowser at Tassili, Algeria
- Cave drawings were found in Iraq depicting dowsing 8,000 years ago
- The writings of Confucius mention dowsing 2,500 B.C. -
- Dowsing tools found in King Tut's tomb are estimated to be 3,300 years old
- Ancient Egyptian stone drawings and carvings show men in exotic headdresses holding forked sticks and pendulums."
- 722 BC - The prophet Hosea of biblical times condemned it. His people had adopted the ways of their captors, including dowsing. He stated, "They consult their piece of wood and their wand makes pronouncements to them."
- In 1,271 Marco Polo returned from his trip to the Orient with detailed information on dowsing.
- In 1,300 a Benedictine monk named Valentine wrote of his experiments with dowsing. He described using six types of rods for locating different metals underground."
- In 1560 Queen Elizabeth of England, imported German miners to teach dowsing to English miners.
- 1990 article in a London newspaper; "The most successful treasure dowser in Britain is Jim Longton from Lancashire. Jim took up dowsing when he retired from the wrestling ring and first hit the headlines in 1990 after finding a spectacular hoard of Viking silver brooches valued at over £40,000. ($60,000)"

Today's dowsing methods may have originated in Germany during the 15th century, when it was used in locating metal ore.

In 1518 Martin Luther listed dowsing for metals as an act that broke the first commandment (*i.e.*, as occultism). The 1550 edition of Sebastian Münster's *Cosmographia* contains a woodcut of a dowser with forked rod in hand walking over a cutaway image of a mining operation. The rod is labelled "Virgula Divina –

Dowsing for metal ore, from 1556 "De re metallica libri XII" book

Glück rüt" (Latin: divine rod; German "Wünschelrute": fortune rod or stick), but there is no text accompanying the woodcut.

By 1556 Georgius Agricola's treatment of mining and smelting of ore, *De Re Metallica*, included a detailed description of dowsing for metal ore. In the sixteenth century, German deep mining technology was in enormous demand all over Europe and German miners were licensed to live and work in Elizabethan England particularly in the Stannaries of Devon & Cornwall and in Cumbria.

Dowsing Rod – Holy Church Property
In the sixteenth or seventeenth centuries the Church claimed the dowsing rod as holy Church property. Theodore Besterman in *Water Divining*, pages 188 and 189, tells of the Holy Mass instituted to be read over the rod before allowing it to be used by an outsider. After the Mass, the rod was to be held in the hands and these words intoned, *"Dowsing Rod, I adjure you in the name of God the Father, the Son, and the Holy*

4

Ghost." Then the rod would work.

Francis Hitching, on page 49 of *Pendulum* remarks that it was common during this time in Germany for the rod to be "Christianized" by placing it in the bed of a newly baptized child, after which the rod was addressed first in the names of the Father, the Son, and the Holy Ghost, then in the child's name, roughly translated, *"that thou tell me so pure and true as Mary the Virgin was, who bore our Lord Jesus Christ, how many fathoms it is from here to the ore"* after which the stick held in the hands would answer by nodding a certain number of times indicating the number of fathoms.

This is exactly the method used today except the rod answers in feet, and it does not have to be addressed in the name of the Father etc. Hitching goes on to say that one of the problems of the Church at that time was that so many of their priests were natural born dowsers.

The Dowsing Tools

Most experienced or professional dowsers use all the basic dowsing tools. These are usually the L Rod, Y Rod or V Rod, Pendulum, Aurameter and the Bobber.

A dowsing device can be made on the spot by cutting a clothes hanger into an L-rod or hanging some object, such as your car keys, on a string to create a pendulum.

Dowsing devices come in all sizes, shapes and materials. It doesn't seem to matter very much to most experienced dowsers what the dowsing tool is made of. Although many dowsers have their favorites and some even swear by a particular tool that works well for them, it appears that all the dowsing tools seem to work equally well.

Lessons in Dowsing

Choose a comfortable, quiet place, where you can be alone for practice on a daily basis, preferably the same time each day. Relax, become quiet and drift into a prayerful mood (alpha state). This is important in the beginning as you begin teaching yourself to dowse.

L- Rods

How to Use: Hold loosely in your hand with the top wire tilted slightly downward. When one L Rod is used alone, it acts as a pointer or a swing rod. It can be requested to point towards a target or direction, or to swing sideways when encountering a specified energy field.

L-Rods can also point in a direction when searching for an object. L-Rods can be used for locating water, treasure, people, food, directions and information. L-Rods are useful for any type of dowsing.

Curl your fingers and thumb around the short leg of your "L" rods. The rods should not touch your hands in any way while holding them. It is critical that they be free to swing without interference.

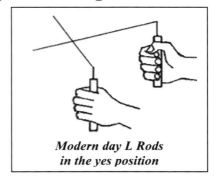

Modern day L Rods in the yes position

Place your elbows along the side of your body for stability, and extend your lower arms and the rods straight out pointing forward. You should ideally hold the rods level for maximum movement and sensitivity, though you may drop the tips of the rods very slightly to dampen the movement in breezy conditions for more control.

For answers to questions: repeat the "Show Me" questions you used for the pendulum. The answers

6

will be: Show me Yes – the rods will cross, Show me No – the rods swing away, Show me Maybe – One rod will swing inward.

Finding Direction or Pointing to Objects

Using a single rod ask your question. For example, standing on a sandy beach you ask, "In which direction should I travel to find the most treasure?" Your single rod will swing one-way or another.

You can test your rod by asking it to point to someone in your party; where is Bob? The single rod should swing and point to Bob. This particular feature can come in very handy. Perhaps you return after a lengthy search only to find someone ate your lunch! What do you do? You ask the rods "Point to the person who ate my lunch today."

Advantages: Easy to make. Easy to use and are very versatile. Works well when walking over rough terrain. They are generally not affected by mild winds.

Disadvantage: Not as easy to carry or conceal as a pendulum

These are made of metal, and may have loosely fitted tube handles which allow the arms of the rods to move freely. L- rods can be made with any metal with Bronze "welding" rods being very popular. You can make a set of L-rods from coat-hanger wire.

To use, hold one rod in each hand, short part of the L held in the hand and the long part of the L pointing forward.

Walk if they turn to the right, the dowser walks to the right. If they turn to the left, the dowser walks to the left. When the dowser passes over or near the searched-for material, the two rods will either cross or uncross. If the rods stop pointing straight ahead and form an "X," the dowser marks the spot. The field may be walked several times, confirming the marked spot until the dowser is satisfied that the L-rods have

7

accurately presented the sought-for item.

Amongst the many things rods can provide is Yes or
No answers to questions asked. Example: "Are there
valuables buried in the sand on this beach?" The
Rods will answer by swinging to either the Yes or No
position.

The Rods will also point to objects you want to find.
Using just one Rod say; "Point to the direction
valuables can be found on the beach." The single rod
will swing to indicate the direction in which you
should travel.

Switch to Modern Technology
You can then either continue using the rods to
uncover the treasure or switch to a modern day metal
detector to complete the task of discovery. Should you
decide to continue by using the Rods simply hold the
two rods parallel to the ground and walk slowly in the
direction the rods have indicated. The Rods will swing
open when you are over the buried items.

Locate Lost Animals, Children and More
To find the lost animal or child etc simply ask "Where
is Fluffy?" and the single Rod will swing to the
direction you should travel. We were at our cabin in
northern Maine one January with our new puppy. In
the hustle and bustle of unloading the skiing gear,
food, luggage etc, Skipper wandered off somewhere.

We were the only people at the lake on the edge of the
White Mountain National Forest that January. Which
way did Skipper wander? With no one to ask if they
had seen him; which way should we go to find the little
pooch? You guessed it; our "Magic Rods" (L rods)
came to the rescue. Skipper had crossed over the
frozen lake and we found him right where the Rods

indicated; huddled under the porch of a vacant cottage.

Captain Kidd Used "Magic Rods" to Locate Sunken Treasure

In 1588 the defeat of the Spanish Armada brought the Spanish Galley *Florencia* into the harbor of Tobermory Bay in northern Scotland. She was badly damaged during battle and shortly after dropping her anchor in the harbor the ship exploded and sank. Records indicate it was heavily laden with gold and silver, which today would be valued at *Forty Three Million Dollars*, when it went down.

Captain William Kidd, before becoming a famous pirate, was a successful businessman in Glashow, Scotland. Kidd employed a "dowser" from Yorkshire, England to search for the treasure ship *Florencia* of Tobermory Bay.

The dowser was reportedly not only able to locate sunken treasure but could also tell what was being detected by the rods: gold, silver, or copper.

Abbé Le Lorrain de Vallemont, wrote in 1706:
"But, with the divining rod, it is possible to distinguish what metal is contained in the mine towards which the rod inclines. For if a gold coin be placed in each hand, the rod will only turn in the direction of gold, because it becomes impregnated with the corpuscles or minute particles of gold. If silver be treated in the same way, the rod will only dip towards silver. This, at any rate, is what we are told by those who pride themselves on their successful use of the rod."

The very scholarly Abbé Le Lorrain de Vallemont of France who in 1693 published *La Physique Occulte*, or "Treatise on the Divining Rod and its Uses for the Discovery of Springs of Water, Metallic Veins, Hidden

Treasure, Thieves, and Escaped Murderers" is quoted as saying:

"If one desires to find pirates' gold, it is really essential to believe in the divining rod and devoutly obey its magic messages."

Pendulum

Pendulums can be made from surveyors' plumb bobs, crystals, washers or just about anything you can suspend from a chain or string. Favorite among serious treasure hunters is the hollow pendulums that can contain a small sample or "witness" of the item being sought.

Dowsing pendulums, with and without the contained sample, may be taken into the field, but more often they are hung on a chain or bit of string and employed in the practice of map dowsing or remote dowsing.

Advantages : Easy to make with only a string and weight plus it's simple to use. It's also small enough to fit into your pocket or purse. Quick response. Excellent tool for dowsing charts or maps.

Disadvantage: Difficult to use in the wind or when walking. This problem can be overcome by requesting the pendulum to spin in a clockwise or counter-clockwise direction to indicate the "yes" or "no" response.

How to Use: Hold your pendulum's string or chain (1/2 to 3 inches long) between your thumb and first finger. The longer the chain the more dramatic the swing will be. Allow the weight to slide through your fingers until it begins rotating. This is your ideal length for dowsing with this pendulum.

Ask it out loud, with a normal speaking voice, "Show Me YES". The pendulum will begin to swing, usually front and back. If the pendulum does not move then cause it to move by moving your hand. Stop the swing and ask your "show me" question again. Continue until the pendulum swings on its own. Repeat with saying "Show Me NO" and the pendulum will swing from side to side.

"Show me Maybe" will result in your pendulum swinging in a circle. Finally, give the command "Show me Ready." The pendulum returns to a steady perpendicular position.

Don't give up if you unable to accomplish the above in about 15 minutes of trying. Let it rest and try again after awhile or the next day. You can do it, yes you can.

Begin Dowsing

Before beginning a session, with the pendulum in the Ready position, ask: Is it OK to Begin dowsing? If the pendulum goes to "NO", then try again at a later time. If the pendulum swings to "YES", it's time to begin.

Rules to Remember

Dowsing takes every word in a question by its literal meaning. If your question has words that have conflicting meanings, your answer may be misleading.

Rule #I: You need to be very specific about what you want to know. This includes what, where, when and sometimes instructional information relating to the question.

Rule #2: Use only words, phrases and conditions that are specific.

Rule #3: Make the question a definite request for information that exists somewhere. Don't ask for an opinion.

Map Dowsing or Remote Dowsing

Map dowsers use a pendulum, plumb bob, or a single L-rod and a map to locate treasure be it gold, silver, jewelry, coins, oil, minerals, persons, water, old foundations. Basically, map dowsing can be used to help you find essentially anything you can imagine. Remote dowsing can save the dowser hours of searching. It can also allow you to locate missing or lost objects if given a map of a house or the layout of a room.

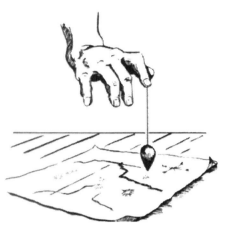

The movement of the pendulum or rod over locations on the map indicates where your objective can be found. Your search on the map begins by asking questions. "Can treasure be found in this area?" The question will be answered either "Yes" or "No". Continue asking questions that will lead to more specific locations that will contain the object of your search.

The map is used as a stand-in for the territory to be

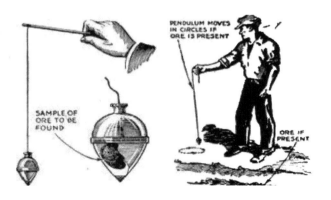

dowsed. The pendulum indicates areas of interest, which may later be searched in person.

Map dowsing is a great way to identify a general area likely to produce good results. Then, narrow down an area to search and avoid walking a grid over a large geographic area.

Where are my car keys? You can use a blueprint or layout of your home or a room to locate missing objects.

Methods for Map Dowsing

Two methods, which seem to be the basics for many variations of remote map dowsing using a dowsing tool, ruler, pencil and a map to remotely target objects on a map.

First – a. Slide a straight edge across a map or drawing, from left to right (after carefully specifying what you are looking for and asking the May I, Can I, Should I) and ask the dowsing device to indicate when the straight edge is at the target.

b. When dowsing device indicates that the straight edge is at the target, draw or sight a line along, the edge.

c. Turn your straight edge 90' and slide it from the bottom towards the top of the map. Ask the dowsing device to indicate when the straight edge is at the target. Draw or sight a  line along the edge, and where your first and second, lines cross will be the target.

13

TIP: If you use a pendulum and chart ask the pendulum to swing a little ways to the left of "YES" and to move closer to "YES" as you move your straight edge (or pencil) closer to the target (treasure, gold, silver, coins, jewelry or object.) "YES" is on target, and swinging to the right of "YES" is past the target.

Second - Ask a pendulum to swing towards a target, and then follow this direction until it spins. Or ask an L Rod to point towards a target and lock on as you move. You can use any of the above or invent your own. With practice all, including your own, will work fine. Have fun.

Move Onto the Field

Armed with the information gained map dowsing you can now travel to your desired hunting spot with confidence of your success.

Y ROD a/k/a Forked Stick

Shape: Traditionally it is a forked stick looking like the letter Y They can be any size, usually around 12 to 24 inches in length.

Material: Can be wood, metal or plastic. Plastic being very common for many dowsers.

How to Use: Hold with pointed end down. Thumbs will be up and palms towards center. Hold tight and spread Y Rod outward while rotating your wrist outward. Your thumbs will now be pointed outward and your palms up. The Y Rod will flip up into a delicate balance. An upward angle of around 45 degrees is usually used for the ready

14

position. Swinging down from the ready position to point at a water vein or target. This may also be used for the "yes" response. Swinging up from the ready position is usually used for the no" response.

Advantages: Acts quickly, can point directly towards a water vein or target. Works well while walking over rough ground. Reliable in fairly strong winds.

Disadvantage: Not as versatile as other dowsing tools. It only has an up and down motion. You will need to turn your body to find direction.

V Rod
The method and technique for using a V-rod are basically the same as for the Y-rod. Simply request the rods to lead you to the object you want to find. Commands to the rods may be out loud or to yourself.

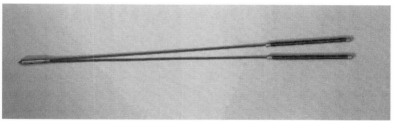
V rod

Allow the rods lead the way. Hold the rods in the same manner as with the Y rod, palms up. Allow the pulls and tugs lead you to the object you are seeking.

Learning to dowse is like learning to play a musical instrument. Practice, practice, practice

BOBBER (Wand, Spring Rod)

Any flexible rod, branch or wire. Can be most any length from one foot to over three feet. They sometimes have a coiled wire and a weighted tip.

Bobber variations

Material: Any thing that is flexible including a thin branch from a tree or shrub.

How to Use: Hold it down at around 45 degrees. The rod will bob up and down for "yes" and sideways for "no" and swing in a circle for "Ready." You may request different bobber responses: swinging back and forth towards a requested target and to spin when over the target.

Advantages: Can replace a pendulum for fieldwork. Most dowsers find it easy to use.

Disadvantages: Won't usually fit in your pocket or purse.

Asking the Right Question Correctly:

The American Society of Dowsers advises: *"Dowsing is very literal and many long time dowsers like to say, "You always get the correct answer. What did you ask for?"*

The key to asking the right question correctly is to first realize that one question is almost never going to get the answer. Often it takes a series of question (often referred to as a Protocol) to get to the answer that the dowser is looking for.

In the case of field dowsing once the dowser has located the vein of water it's important to locate the depth of the vein. This is often done by asking, "is the said vein less than 20'? ... less than 30'?... less than 40'? ...less than 50'?" until an affirmative response is given and the dowser now can ask for depth in single digits (ie. 47'?, 48'?, 49'?).

It is very helpful, when first starting to dowse, to write your questions down before asking.

Writing down your question will allow you to re-write it until you narrow it down specifically before you start dowsing. Rarely is one question enough. Dowsers often develop series of questions, or protocols, for their informational searches."

Again, _dowsing is very literal_ so be careful of how you phrase your questions. For example: You ask the rods to point to North yet they continually point to the East. Why? Perhaps because your friend Tom North is standing east of you and the rods are literally pointing to North, Tom North.

You ask; is it going to rain today? The dowsing device responds yes yet it does not rain. What's wrong? Perhaps the question was answered literally correct and your question not specific enough. It did rain today somewhere in the world.

17

Asking Permission:

Many dowsers feel it's very important to ask permission before starting to dowse. They accomplish this by asking three simple questions: "Can I, May I, Should I?"

The "Can I" question is for ability. Essentially the dowser is asking if they have the ability of do this kind of dowsing. Do they have enough experience to complete the dowsing job they wish to do?

May I? By asking the "May I" question you are asking permission from the "universe". Perhaps this is a task better left undone as the results might end up as detrimental to those involved.

Should I? The "Should I" question asks; ethically speaking, is this a dowsing task that you ought to be involved with?

Thank You Many dowsers feel obligated to give thanks at the end of a session; thanks for the gift they have been given

Dowsing Charts

Once you start learning how to get reliable dowsing answers, you naturally want to expand your use of this amazing ability to give you even more detailed and valuable information. Dowsing is a search for information and answers, after all, and the more you can get, the better. This is where dowsing charts come in handy.

Dowsing charts help you go beyond a simple "yes" or "no" answer. Charts and scales, which are closely related, provide you with the opportunity to have several or more possible answers instead of just two. With this more advanced technique you can pick a specific therapy, supplement or any choice among a range of possibilities. You can assign a number value that represents benefits, intensity or harm.

The ability to find shades of "yes" and shades of "no" and to choose among many options makes dowsing a more valuable tool for everyday life.

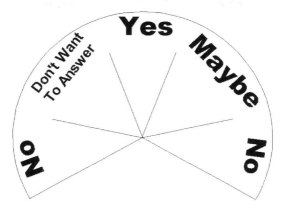

Charts and scales come in many forms. Some are simple and linear in design, while others are complex and include multiple scales or even connect multiple charts to one another.

In general, when using a chart or scale you must do the same as with any dowsing.

1. You need a good dowsing question
2. You must get into a good dowsing state
3. You must be detached and open to the answer

Dowsing is way more than just getting an answer. The answer will only be as accurate as your dowsing technique, and your ability depends on how skillful you are, which all comes down to training and practice.

A dowser will usually use a pendulum for chart dowsing. We have found it helpful if the pendulum has a pointy end, because that makes it easier to see what answer is being indicated on the chart or scale.

Create Your Own Chart

Fill in with the questions you wish to have answered for a custom chart.

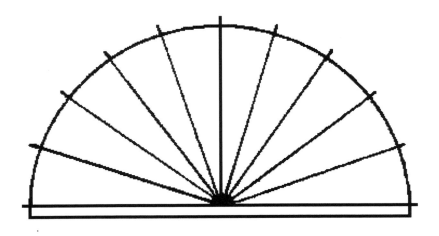

List Dowsing

List dowsing is analogous to chart dowsing, in that you can take the information and put it in a chart, or you can just put it in a list. List dowsing is finding the answer to your dowsing question from a list.

Lists are more useful than charts when you have a lot of options, more options than you can easily chart. The principle behind list dowsing is much the same as chart dowsing.

The list below might be representative of one you would create for map dowsing a beach you are considering to visit.

Rings	Coins	Jewelry	Cash	Valuable Other

Use your Rods/Bobber to determine depth.

Your rods/bobber have indicated that the treasure or whatever else you are dowsing for is in the earth under your feet.
How deep is it?

There are two ways to determine the depth.

First, simply ask your dowsing device. Ask, is it 10 feet, 20 feet, 30 feet etc until your dowsing device signals Yes.

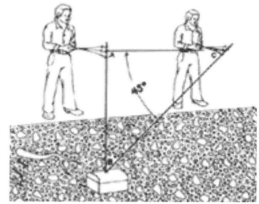
Determine the depth of an object

Second, with the rods crossed, move away from the target. When the rods open mark the spot. Then inch along some more. When the rods close mark that spot. The distance between the spots is the depth.

It should be the same distance you obtained by asking. It certainly is nice to have a second opinion and confirmation before you begin digging.

Where to

Find

Gold, Silver, Coins, Jewelry, Ancient Relics, and other Treasures

Why People Hid/Buried Valuables

People have been hiding money since the beginning of time. More recently, the stock market crash of October 1929 left the American public highly nervous and extremely susceptible to rumors of impending financial disaster. This situation and other economic woes during the Great Depression led to a wave of banking panics or "bank runs," during which large numbers of anxious people withdrew their deposits in cash.

Most banks during the depression were over leveraged and had almost 99% of people's money lent out in car, consumer, and home loans. The "Run on the Bank" phenomenon led to many bank failures.

Understandably, people "once bitten, and twice shy" from the affects of this tough economic time in our country's history.

As a result, people stopped saving their money in the banks, and instead hid their money and valuables in and around their homes and farms.

People hid their money and other valuables for many reasons besides the banking crisis. Not only did some not trust the banks, they just didn't trust people, including their spouse and family.
Others would hide valuables at home because; the bank was a long distance away by horse and buggy, it was more convenient to have it close by, didn't trust the Stock Market. Many individuals hide money just to feel secure.

Unfortunately many would die without disclosing to anyone where their fortune was hidden.

Finding Treasure Around Your Home

Where Did People Like to Hide Valuables in Earlier Times?

If you live in an older home or have access to explore in one, the following will information should be of interest and value to you.

More than twenty years ago, a treasure hunter named Michael Paul Henson wrote *"27 Unusual Places to Look for Treasure,"* an article that you can still find online. Here are some of the places where he reported that he had found hidden valuables:

- Above false closet ceilings
- Behind loose bricks around fireplaces and elsewhere
- Behind wallpaper (look for bulges)
- Between layers of shelf paper (popular for paper currency)
- Buried in flower gardens
- In hollowed-out beams and/or logs in log cabins
- Inside couch and chair cushions
- Inside door locks
- Inside hollow bed posts (a popular place to stash gold coins, Henson wrote)
- Inside hollowed-out fence and clothesline posts
- Inside hollowed-out stones placed outdoors
- Inside old chicken coops (Henson notes that chickens made "good watchdogs")
- Inside or surrounding fireplace cleanouts
- Sewn into carriage seats and horse harnesses
- Under false bottoms in feed bins in barns
- Under paving stones
- Under porch floors
- Under siding and shingles
- Under steps
- Under window sills and casements
- Behind loose stones or bricks in foundations

- Behind mantles made of slate and other materials
- Down wells (coins or gold jewelry could be placed in a box and lowered down using a rope)
- In outhouses, barns and sheds
- In safes hidden behind closet walls or under closet floors
- Inside tool cabinets and toolboxes
- Under floorboards

Most productive places in and around your house or apartment to find valuables.

Garage - The garage is a common hiding place for all sorts of things. Look in the rafters, in the attic if there is one, and in any and all cabinets and containers.

In 2012, Carson City, Nevada, officials made some interesting discoveries while inspecting a house left behind by a recluse who died with no nearby relatives. They found $12,000 in cash in the house, but soon that amount looked paltry. In the garage, neatly wrapped in aluminum foil, was **$7 million in gold coins.**

Check out any old toolboxes you find in the garage. Some tools might be sold as useful items or, if they are old and interesting, as collector's items.

Then there are the other things that sometimes get left in a toolbox. Consider the man in England who one day looked through his deceased father's old toolbox and found a handful of old coins **he later auctioned for $50,000.**

Backyard - Valuable discoveries in yards are not uncommon. In early 2014, while hiking out of their backyard, a California couple found a buried treasure **worth $10 million:** six metal cans, each one filled with rare gold coins.

A metal detector can help you find buried valuables. Hidden currency is often in a container made partially of metal, like a jar with a metal top. Burying things under the edge of a cement walkway or driveway is also common.

Garbage and Recycling Bins - Excited that the dealers from "Antiques Road show" were coming to his town, a man brought in a violin he had plucked from someone's trash. Maybe it was worth a little something, he thought. As it turned out, once cleaned up, his junk-picked violin was **worth around $50,000.** Apparently it was a creation of Giuseppe Pedrazzini, a famous Italian violinmaker.

If you see something interesting sticking out of a neighbor's trashcan, why not grab it? It's fair game once it's discarded. If you live in a condo development, watch that dumpster for treasures. Condo residents tend to generously put anything of value alongside the dumpster instead of in it.

Garden - Soil is already loosened, so a garden is an easy place to bury things. Use your dowsing skills or metal detector to avoid having to dig up the whole garden. If you can find old photos of your home, you might discover parts of the yard that used to be a garden, and search these spots.

Gardens can be wild places, and sometimes things get lost in the weeds. Coins and tools fall from the pockets of gardeners, and on occasion even statues get lost. Wait... statues? That's right — a man in England **found a statue** worth $33,000 behind overgrown bushes in his garden.

Barns and Sheds - Barns, sheds, and other outbuildings around a home are natural places to hide things, and good places to continue your treasure hunt. You might find valuable items left behind by previous owners.

People also purposely hide things in outbuildings. A plastic peanut butter jar, filled with old silver coins, was found under loose cement tiles of a tool shed.

Old pump houses are another place to investigate. In years past, because people didn't trust banks as much, they would hide gold/silver coins in false water lines. Look for pipes that don't actually go anywhere or do not connect to others.

Who knows what might be out there in your shed or barn?

Foundations - Treasure hunters look at foundation remaining at old homesteads to determine where the front steps and porch would have been. Why? That's where people most often sat down to rest, so it's also where coins most often fell out of pockets and got lost in the grass and dirt.

If your own home is old enough, there might be some **valuable coins** where people sat generations ago. Get out your dowsing stuff or metal detector and shovel.

Success Stories – A California couple found a stash of rare gold coins hidden in a rusty can under a tree while walking their dog. The coins have been valued at more than $10 million.

In 1990, a couple armed with metal detectors found an extremely rare 1652 New England sixpence coin in a potato field. That coin sold for $431,250 at auction.

In 2012, a New Mexico boy used a metal detector to locate a two-pound meteorite. The meteorite likely would bring thousands of dollars if sold.

Single finds that yield millions of dollars are extremely rare. However, amateur treasure hunters can dig up antique bottles, lost coins and jewelry. Interesting artifacts such as military relics from Revolutionary War or Civil War battles or Native American arrow heads from thousands of years ago that are still waiting to be found.

Your chances of success are multiplied because, not only can you employ a metal detector, but you also have the ancient art of dowsing at your disposal.

15 Best Treasure Hunting Sites

There are literally hundreds of places to find coins, rings, jewelry, gold, relics, and even real buried and hidden treasures.

The key to finding treasures/valuables is to go where people have been, where they lived, where they worked and played. Research as far back as you can to identify such sites. Old-time ball fields, carnival and circus sites hold great potential for finding valuables that were lost long ago. <u>People lose coins, rings, jewelry, and other treasures everywhere they go.</u>

All sorts of valuables are lost or hidden for safekeeping. Many valuables and treasures are buried by owners who perhaps die and never come back to retrieve them. All these millions of coins and tens of thousands of dollars in rings and jewelry are out there waiting to be found! With the right tools and proper research, you could be the "lucky" one.

Some of the best places to search:

- Parks
- Schoolyards, Playgrounds
- Fairgrounds
- Picnic Areas
- Amusement Parks
- Swimming Areas such as Lakes and Rivers
- Seaside Beaches
- Sand, Dirt or Grassy Parking Areas
- Old Home Sites
- Old School Sites
- Under Grandstands and Bleachers
- Churchyards
- Stonewalls near old farmhouses
- Cemeteries
- Carnival Sites
- Abandoned houses

Finding Treasure in Strange Places

Old Cars - Many old timers used the gas tanks of their abandoned vehicles to stash their coins.

An example: An enterprising young man purchased an old farm. The farm had two old automobiles from the early 1920's abandoned in the scrub brush on the property.

When this individual was moving one of the old wrecks from the property, and as he was lifting the old tank from the frame of the wreck he heard a clanking sound inside the gas tank. At the same time the rusted bottom of the tank fell to the ground, and with it was a cache of Barber coins.

Amazed at this discovery, the young man began searching for other old abandoned wrecks, hoping for the same situation. He reported that in three years he had located fifteen old, abandoned wrecks, and three of them had coins cached in their old gas tanks.

Hollowed Out Old Trees - A man purchased a home that had not been lived in for many years.

He was working the back of the property in a thick area populated with old elm and maple trees. One of the old trees had a large hollowed hole in the center of the trunk, about four feet from the ground. He spotted a piece of burlap bag hanging from inside the hollowed out area.

Inside the hollowed tree trunk was a rotted, old, burlap bag that contained old coins dating between 1832 and 1877.

Beneath Old Bridges - Why were the bridges used as hiding spots for money? Reason: gangsters used the old, back roads, to travel after committing their robbery. The bridges that crossed the rivers and streams were great hiding places.

The steel joists, or old wooden girders on their undersides were perfect places to store a cache of money or valuables. Perhaps today's modern thieves on the run, like drug dealers, also use the old bridges as caching locations. Many times the bad guy gets caught, and is thrown into prison before having a chance to go back to his cache.

Cold Cellars - Just about every old homestead had a

cold storage cellar. This was an area where the property owners stored their food. These holes in the ground were nothing more than a small cellar hole lined with the rock from the area.

Many times these cold cellar have produced caches of all kinds for the treasure hunter interested enough to search for them.

Near The Well - Another popular area where treasures have been located is near a well. The well was used often and it was a perfect place to bury or drop a treasure. Most wells were also located behind the homes, so it would be secretive and easy to hide valuables time and time again.

Outhouse

The Outhouse - They can hold a wealth of valuables from old pottery, bottles, buttons, coins, and yes-even treasures.

There have been treasures found inside outhouses, as well s beneath the wooden thrones. One individual located an old metal container fastened beneath the throne, held there by a few nails and a metal strip. Inside the container were hundreds of silver dollars dating from the mid 1800's.

You might want to check out the outhouse with your dowsing or metal detecting equipment before diving in.

Eight Great, "Beyond the Beach," Search Areas

Among the places worth searching that many treasure hunters overlook or fail to consider include:

The strip of land between roads and sidewalks is one such place. Coins, jewelry and other items dropped by people walking along sidewalks or taking out their car keys can end up in this soil. If the road is old, there even could be items lost by people riding horses in past centuries.

Forgotten picnic grounds. The local historical society or library might be able to direct you to old picnic grounds, or they might have old photos, letters, journals or local histories that provide clues that you can use to find these places.

Old picnic sites are wonderful places to search because people sat on the ground and engaged in sporting activities there, both of which often cause small valuables to fall out of pockets and get lost in the soil.

Old public parks. Parks that have been in use for decades can be wonderful search sites for the same reasons as picnic grounds. Most parks already have been picked over by other treasure hunters, however, so concentrate your search on sections of parks that other treasure hunters often overlook.

These include overgrown areas, which might not have been overgrown in past decades...and the trails into and out of the parks, which tend to be ignored by treasure hunters hurrying to get to the main park grounds.

Stonewalls In and under old stonewalls. People sometimes stash things in stonewalls and then never return to retrieve them.

Vacant lots where buildings stood in the distant past. To find these, visit local libraries and historical societies and ask if they have old maps of your area that show building locations. Compare these to present-day maps of the area, such as the satellite maps available on Google Maps.

Around old swimming holes. Swimmers often dropped coins and jewelry when they changed clothes near swimming holes. Search not only around the water's edge but also in nearby overgrown spots that could potentially have provided cover for changing clothes.

Riverbanks and lake shorelines are excellent spots to search for Native American artifacts, since that's where they made their camps. These items, spear tips, arrowheads or axe heads generally are made of stone, not metal, so here is where your dowsing equipment and skills will come in handy..

Dried-up bodies of water. When the water level falls in draught-stricken reservoirs, lakes or rivers, search the newly exposed land. You might find items lost by swimmers or boaters...or even old guns discarded by criminals (guns are especially likely in bodies of water near cities).

Rural home/farm dumps Municipal trash collection was not always available in the country, so people just created their own dumps somewhere out of the way on their own property. Do a little digging—it might be a dump, and you might find some unexpected treasures. Items once discarded as trash now are collectible and valuable. For example, antique bottles are a very common abandoned dump find. The best place to find antique bottles is in old trash dumps

Finding Relics and Old Coins

Recovering older more valuable coins plus holding different relics of the past in your hands will be something you will want to experience. Finding coins from the 17th, 18th and early 19th Century is a far greater thrill then you can imagine.

The answer to finding older sites is "Research!" Where can you find research material?

1-Old Maps - can be found in local libraries, local history books, they show old roads, abandoned railroad stations, many times school buildings and other points of interest that either no longer exist, or people have forgotten about.

2-Old Newspapers contain a wealth of information on almost every page Stories about holiday celebration on the town square park (May no longer exists) Carnival arriving in town (where did they set up?) and much more information.

3-Old Property Tax Records show where older houses, farms, service stations, interstate bus stops, taverns etc, once stood.

4-Local Historical Societies are a great resource containing valuable information on dozens of older happenings of your town from its very beginnings up till today.

5-Local Museums usually have displays of historical interest as well as many books on the area's history. Spend time with anyone that works in the museum, they generally are part "Historian."

6- Librarians can direct you to a wealth of information about your town. Libraries are the main "Depository" of information of all kinds,, many times having a number of items discussed above, "old maps, old books, old records, etc".

Finding Treasure on Beaches

As you know, beaches are popular places to use metal detectors. A long seaside beach is an ideal place to combine ancient and modern treasure hunting devices and technology.

Dowse then Metal Detect

You are standing on a National Seashore beach on Cape Cod. You know that the shifty shoals just off shore were the site of hundreds of shipwrecks over the centuries. In fact, before the Cape Cod Canal was opened, this section of the Cape was referred to as the "Graveyard of the Atlantic."

Found on the beach

Artifacts, jewelry, coins and other valuables are continually being washed ashore by Nor'easters and frequent Atlantic storms.

The beach extends for several miles in each direction. Which way should travel to find your treasure? This is where your dowsing abilities come in handy. You ask your dowsing devise, "Which direction should I go to find valuable items?" Your rods react and point out to sea. They are probably pointing to one of the ancient shipwrecks and its sunken cargo.

You remember that dowsing devises respond to question very literally. You didn't bring your scuba gear so you rephrase the question. "In which direction should I travel to find valuables <u>on the beach</u>?"

The rods react and point down the beach. The beach is miles long. It would be nice to know how far you have to go so you ask; "How far away – more than 10 yards – 20, 30, etc until you have your answer.

You can choose to complete the entire search without using your metal detector using your dowsing equipment alone. In fact, certain sections of the Cape's National Seashore do not allow metal detectors on the beach. Especially the section of the beach where the sunken pirate treasure ship, the Whydah, went down in April of 1717 is located. It lies 1,500 feet offshore in thirty feet of water. Several tons of treasure has been salvaged with more remaining to be brought up.

Treasure from the beach

Walking this beach carrying an innocent necklace (pendant) directing your travel probably would be ok and not attract much attention. Or is a pendant, (necklace) a metal detector? Hmmm.

Beachgoers often lose coins, watches and jewelry in the sand, and tides and storms pull items lost at sea and from shipwrecks back to shore.

Valuables found on the beach may have been dropped by a vacationer or washed ashore from a sunken ship. Beach hunting is probably the only form of treasure hunting where almost anyone can go and find items worth $100's or even $1,000's without the aid of fancy equipment. Sometimes all it takes to find a beach treasure is a keen eye.

How to Pan For Gold

When you pan for gold you are going to want a gold pan and some gravel with lead shot or BBs to simulate the gold (flatten the lead shot)

Panning for Gold

Fill a tub with water to do the panning in. Put some gravel in your gold pan, but not too much, start small.

1. Completely lower your pan into a tub of water.
2. Shake your pan in the water to turn your gravel 'soupy'. Don't spill any out yet.
3. Tilt your pan slightly and wash water in and out, gravel should be carried out with the water.
4. After washing out some gravel, level out your pan again and shake it some more.
5. Repeat this process until just the heaviest black sands and gold remain.
6. Swirl water across the black sands and tap the edge of your pan to help separate the gold from sand.

Gold Panning takes practice to get good at but it's a fun and rewarding activity.

The Mechanics of Panning for Gold

When you put some gravel in your pan with water, the gold will be the heaviest thing in the pan. If you are in a stream or river, take your shovel and dig some material from the bottom and place it in your pan. You can use a classifier to sift out the larger material. The

Classifier

objective is to get the gold to the bottom of your pan and wash the sand and gravel out. Place the pan in water get all the material in the pan moving around. There is no right or wrong way to pan. Just do what works the best for you.

To remove the sand and gravel, hold both sides of the pan and move it from side to side quickly to loosen the sand and allow the gold to settle to the bottom of the pan. This is called stratification.

To get the sand and gravel out move the pan front to back bringing water into the pan on the forward motion, and floating the lighter materials off on the backward motion. Let the water wash only the top layer of sand out of the pan keeping the material on the bottom motionless.

Steepen the angle each time you shake to bring additional material to the top to wash off. REMEMBER to stratify Use a side-to-side motion (Stratify) twice as much as front to back (wash). Gold will begin to show as you wash the black sand off of it. Remember the gold is heavy. It will be under all of the black sand on the very bottom of the pan. If you shook and washed correctly it will stay in the pan. Tap the 12:00 o'clock (top) of the pan with your thumb to make the gold jump farther into the side.

As with most everything – Practice makes Perfect – Good Luck

Finding Treasure in
Maine

Where it has been found and *Where you can find more*

Treasure in Maine

Shipwrecks
Shipwrecks along the outer Cape and the rocky coast of Maine are what legends are made of. Thousands of ships, and their crews, have met their end on the shifting sands of Cape Cod, for centuries known as the "Graveyard of The Atlantic." The icy cold waters of the rocky coast of Maine has claimed its share of hapless ships and seamen as well.

Each of these ships and every one of the mariners carried valuables, and in the case of pirates; gold, silver, jewelry, diamonds, rubies etc.

Pirates
It is less likely however, to see a title such as "Pirates

and Treasure in Maine." It is not usual to associate pirates with Maine – pirates were in the warm Caribbean – not in the foggy, cold waters of Maine – or were they?

We have chronicled for you the many pirates, famous and not so famous, that have plied the coast of Maine for centuries. Who were the pirates of Maine? Why were they here? What might they have left behind, and why?

Treasure
Tales of where the pirates have buried their loot and places where some of it has been found are told in these pages. Has all the treasure been found?

Gold, Silver and Jewels were not only buried by pirates but by merchant, farmers and others all over Maine.

Why? - Because banks and other institutions were either not available, or not trusted.

There's gold in them there streams! Yes, gold and valuable gems can be found in some of Maine's many streams and other locations. You may be surprised how accessible the valuable deposits are. We tell you where you might begin your search and find your own treasure.

Pirates Booty

All along the Maine coast are more islands than can be counted, and many of these have been suggested as sites for buccaneers and privateers such as Captain Kidd, Captain Bellamy, and their ilk to have buried treasure.

There are many stories of treasure being lost or buried along the coast of Maine. Many people have tried to find these lost treasures. How true are these stories? After only a little research I have found at least one truly plausible claim. According to Charles M. Skinner who wrote "Myths and Legends of Our Own Land", notorious pirate Captain William Kidd buried treasure in several locations.

Kidd's History

Kidd started off in the Royal Navy fighting against the French. Later he became a pirate hunter for the colonies in the Americas. In 1896, Skinner wrote that there was a spot in Maine near the Piscataqua River where Captain Kidd buried gold and other valuables taken during his time hunting pirates for the crown. It is likely that he wouldn't have turned everything over to the authorities.

Possible Treasure Locations

Another possible hiding place for his accumulated treasure is an island off the coast of Maine called Monhegan Island. Skinner claims that there is a cave on the island where the treasure is. However, Kidd allegedly killed one of his own crew in the cave so that

the ghost of the crewman would haunt the island and protect his treasure. It is said that when some treasure hunters went looking for it that the ghost pulled the treasure deeper into the earth so they couldn't get to it.

There are also other stories of Kidd's treasures in Maine. One says that he sunk some of his treasure into a saltwater lake along the Kennebec River. Another says that he buried treasure on Damariscotta Island. Skinner says that Kidd booby-trapped that part of the river so that no boats could get near the spot where he dropped his treasure. Another possible spot for Captain Kidd's treasure is Appledore, which is in the Isles of Sholes. This place is also said to have some of his slain crew members guarding the hidden treasure.

If you are thinking of treasure hunting in Maine, these would be good places to start. It is likely that at least one of these stories is true and may still **hold long lost valuables.**

Finding Treasure on Maine Islands

Favorite among scores of pirates

Maine Islands Rumored to Have Hidden Treasure

The islands of Maine represent a lifetime of opportunity to find treasure. Pirates have used the many islands to sequester their loot, resume pirating and return, sometimes with a fleet of captured ships, to collect their plunder before returning to Europe to live like kings.

Some of the better known pirates who may have buried their treasure on Maine Islands were: Dixie Bull, Blackbeard (Edward Teach), 'Black' Sam Bellamy, Jack Quelch, William Kidd, Ned Low and some lesser known and unknown pirates as well.

Other islands were trading posts, farms and fishing communities and, as was the custom lacking banks to safeguard their money and gold, people would bury their valuables in the ground for safety. Unfortunately for family but fortunate for us, many would die taking the location of their buried valuables to the grave with them.

Cushing

Damariscove Islands

Appledore Island

Boon Island

Duck Island

Matinicus Island

Damariscotta Island

Monhegan Island

Manana Island

Jewell Island

Baily Island,

Pond Island

Cliff Island

Haskell Island

Orrs Island,

Elm Island

Great Chebeague Island

John's Island

Deer Isle, and Isle Au Haut.

Monroe Island

Oak Island,

Vinalhaven

Outer Heron Island

Hollowell Island,

Twobush Island,

Pittston Island,

Cushing and Damariscove Islands

Maine's First Pirate – 1631 - Dixie Bull, an English sea captain descended from an aristocratic family, was the first pirate known to prey upon shipping off the northeastern colonies, especially along the rocky coast of Maine. Some of his hidden hoards

Pirate Dixie Bull attacks shipping

have contributed to the traditions of pirates and buried treasure along the New England coast.

One of his treasures was reputed to be worth $400,000 at the time of its burial on Damariscove Island. If found today, its value could be worth $4,000,000 or more in today's dollars.

Another of his hoards is supposed to have been buried on Cushing Island, also off the Maine coast. Neither treasure trove is known to have been recovered.

Bull was a native of London who came to Boston in 1631. He was associated with Sir Ferdinando Gorges in development of a large land grant east of Agamonticus at York, Maine. He rapidly adapted to the rugged life of the New Worlds wilderness, becoming a trader in beaver pelts with the Indians.

In June 1631, while trading in the Penobscot Bay area, Bull was attacked by a roving band of Frenchmen in a pinnace, or small sailing ship. They seized his sloop and stock of coats, rugs, blankets, biscuits, etc. This same band captured the Plymouth Company's Castine trading post which was filled with other valuable loot.

Trader Bull, fired by a desire for revenge, assembled 20 men to prey upon French shipping in an effort to recoup his loss. Their attempts were unsuccessful, for the French had temporarily ceased their raids. Bull's food and supplies were running low, so he attacked and plundered three small English vessels in order to keep operating.

Dixie Bull

These attacks put him in serious trouble with the Crown, and he became desperate. His next escapade was later in 1632, when he sailed into the harbor of Pemaquid, sacked the trading post and nearby dwellings, and escaped with $2,500 in both.

There was little resistance to the attack, but while loading goods aboard his sloop, someone on shore fired a musket and Bulls second in command was struck in the chest, killing him. Until then, many of the crew had considered piracy a lark. Now it suddenly became deadly serious business.

Early in February 1633, three of Bull,s crew secretly returned to their Maine homes. They said Bull had sailed eastward and joined the French, his former enemies. Another statement by a Captain Roger Clap indicated that Bull eventually returned to England. His destiny is lost in the maze of history. One version says that he was finally captured and hung at Tyburn, England.

Bull's fate will probably never be known. The fate of his buried treasure on Cushing and Damariscove Islands may be determined by a skillful treasure hunter.

Fort Pemaguid

The Pirate Dixie Bull began his piratical career by converting his trading sloop into a pirate ship and attacking the fort and got loot valued at 500 pounds.

This little-known treasure was found by accident and then lost again and has never been rediscovered

Appledore Island

A Pirate's Ghost Guards the Treasure

Appledore Island is the largest of the Isles of Shoals and is located seven miles off the Maine/New Hampshire coast. It is part of the Town of Kittery and reachable in season by ferry.

Captain Kidd is perhaps one of the most famous pirates in history. He is suspected of hiding treasure from Key West to Maine; more treasure than anyone else. Some of his hidden treasure has been found; most has not.

"Old Bab"

Appledore is reportedly one of his more famous hiding places. Legend has Kidd murdering one of his crew so that he would haunt the hiding place and scare away any possible discoverers.

48

The ghost has been named "Old Bab" and has reportedly been seen by many islanders. They say he has a red ring around his neck, wears tattered clothing and that a phosphorescence glow surrounds his "body."

Boon Island

The Blood Red Rubies of Boon Island

Boon Island is a barren piece of land located in the Gulf of Maine 6 miles off the town of York. The island is very small being only approximately 300' by 700' in size..

On September 25, 1710, the English ship *Nottingham* departed her home port of London and headed for New England. The 120-ton Galley was crewed by fourteen men and carried ten cannon and was commanded by Captain Jonathan Dean. Her cargo consisted of: loads of cordwood, butter and cheese from Ireland, plus one very special cargo, a packet of twelve blood-red rubies in the charge of agent Winthrop Sloan, the sole passenger aboard.

Red rubies

Only in America

The rubies were sold to a wealthy French aristocrat, the Count de Florent, on the condition that they be rendered into matching items of jewelry that matched those of a large pendant and brooch he owned. The Count insisted that the only person in the world capable of performing the task was a goldsmith living in America so off to America went the precious rubies.

The rubies were quite large and carefully packed into an oblong metal box measuring one inch by one-half inch by twelve inches. The box was then securely stored in the ships iron safe. The stones estimated market value today would be well in excess of $2,500,000.

As the *Nottingham* approached New England she was firmly gripped by blinding December snowstorm and a

Ship heading for the rocks

full-force gale. The heavy wind threatened to capsize the ship, so Captain Dean ordered the sails dropped. However, before the task could be completed, a huge wave lifted the galley and plunged it against the eastern end of the jagged, exposed rock known as Boon Island.

Miraculously everyone had survived the sinking, including the passenger Sloan. As the splintered *Nottingham* and her ruby treasure vanished beneath the boiling waves, the men settled into prayer, grateful for their very survival.

Stranded on Boon Island

They had spent twenty-seven days on the rock known as Boon Island before they were rescued. The men were weak and frozen after nearly a month without fresh water, little food, and no fire in the blistering cold. They were walking skeletons. All had frost bite and frozen limbs but they were still alive although many had to have limbs amputated

So there remains, somewhere near Boon Island near Star Island, the scattered wreckage of the *Nottingham,* close nearby, is an iron safe containing a fortune in rare rubies waiting for some lucky person to find them.

Duck Island

Lone Survivor Tells of Money Chest

In March 1876, only one person survived a shipwreck on an unidentified brig that crashed behind White Island. The schooner *Birkmyre* hit Duck Island in March 1875, losing two of its crew and a substantial amount of money in a chest that has not been recovered

Matinicus Island

Pirate Island

Matinicus Island - Often referred to as the *pirate* island because; in the spring of 1717 the pirate ships *Anne*

and *Fisher,* being survivors of the fierce storm of April 26, 1717 that that sank pirate Samuel Bellamy's treasure laden ship the *Whydah* off of a Cape Cod beach.

They were part of the pirate Black Sam Bellamy's fleet and had come north to await Bellamy's arrival after he finished visiting his love, Goody Hallett.

They took over the island used it as their base to attack vessels in the area as they awaited Bellamy's arrival.

While the pirates were at Matinicus it is recorded:

> "....... *they took a sloop belonging to Colonel [Stephen] Minot, one shallop belonging to Capt. [John] Lane and three Schooners. They brought the Sloop and Shallop and (as we are informed) the sails and compasses of the 3 schooners to Menhagen [Monhegan], whereupon they manned the last mentioned Sloop with ten hands...*"

The pirates departed the area on May 9, 1717, on the 25-ton sloop formerly belonging to Colonel Minot, with a pirate crew of 19.

Did they leave part of their loot buried somewhere island for safe keeping until they were able to return?

Damariscotta Island

Kennebec - There is a lake of salt water on the island which, like dozens of shallow ones in this country, is locally reputed to be bottomless.

The notorious pirate captain Kidd is believed to have sunk some of his valuables in this lake. He is reported to have guarded against the entrance of boats by hanging a chain from one side of the narrow entrance to the other.

Others report he booby-trapped the entrance to protect his loot. Key to finding the spot would start by locating the remains of bolts in the rocks and hopefully, traces on both sides of a channel or opening.

Somewhere at the bottom of this lake is the treasure chest sunk by captain Kidd and reportedly protected by a piratical ghost.

Monhegan Island

Treasure Protected by Spirits

Being located miles out to sea off the mainland, Monhegan Island is a natural for pirates. Captain Bellamy, "the richest pirate," is said to have hidden some of his treasure "somewhere on the island"

Ghost of a protective pirate?

On the island there is a cave, opening to the sea, where it is whispered that treasure had been stored in care of ghostly spirits. The party was aware of the spirit curse and knew they must remain perfectly silent so as not to alert the spirits to their presence.

They found within the cave a heavy chest, which they were about to lift when one of the party, contrary to orders whispered; "We've got it!"

The spell was broken, for the watchful spirits heard and snatched away the treasure. Some years ago the

Treasure in a cave

cave was enlarged by blasting, in a hope of finding that chest, for an old saying has been handed down among the people of the island—from whom it came they have forgotten—that was to this effect: "Dig six feet and you will find iron; dig six more and you will find money."

Manana Island

A Pot of Gold

Manana Island is an island in Lincoln County lying adjacent to Monhegan island, about 10 miles off Pemaquid Point.

Around 1900, several fishermen stopped their boat at this island to relax. They decided to play a game of soccer. When a wild kick was made by one of the crewmembers, the captain of the group ran to retrieve the ball.

As he picked up the ball, he noticed rusty metal sticking out of the sand. He dug the sand from around the object, and saw that it was an old iron pot filled with coins. Since he was out of sight of his crew, he stuck the pot into a nearby rock crevice, intending to come back for it later.

After playing for a while longer, the crew went back to their fishing boat. The captain made an excuse to stay behind for a short time. Returning to what he thought was the crevice where he had put the pot of coins, he was amazed that he could not find the right one. Deciding that part of the coins would be better than none, the captain called his crew and told them what he had done.

The entire company spent several hours in search of the coins, but were never able to find them. As far as is known, somewhere on Manana Island, stuck in a rock crevice, there is a cache of coins waiting for a lucky treasure hunter.

Richmond Island

Indians killed traders who had buried their Gold

The island is located offshore from Cape Elizabeth, and the place where a farmer and his two sons found a treasure of gold and silver coins as they plowed their field.

The cache is believed to have belonged to Walter Bagnall (a/k/a 'Great Walt') and his companion John Peverly who, lived on Richmond Island beginning in

Buried jar of treasure

1628. They made their living by trading liquor and English weapons for beaver hides and dried fish with the Sagamore Indians

Bagnall was dishonest in his methods of trading with the Indians and had made huge profits from it. He was described as a 'wicked fellow'.

Squidrayset, the Sagamore sachem, lead the trading negotiations with Bagnall. He was also the sachem who deeded land in Falmouth, Maine to the English settlers.

Winthrop's Journal states that on 3 Oct 1631 *"The Sagamore Indian, Squidrayset and his company massacred and robbed them and burned the Trading Post down around them because they felt they were cheated. They took their guns and anything else that they wanted."*

Men had gone after the murderers but did not catch them. They did, however, get information from friendly Indians as to who it was who killed Bagnall and Peverly. About January of 1633 Captain Neal had gone after pirates but returned, as it was so cold they could not follow them.

They went to Richmond Island where they found and hung the Indian Black Will, one of those who had murdered Walter Bagnall.

Squidrayset is the man who killed Walter Bagnall & his companion John Peverly. However the Indian Manatahqua was hanged instead. The records agree that Bagnall deserved his fate and that Manatahqua did not.

It was much later in the year 1855 when the farmer and his two sons unearthed the jar of treasure. In the jar they found 21 gold coins, 31 silver coins dated as early as 1602 from the crowns of Europe, and a gold signet ring with the initials 'G.V.' Some reports speculate that this 'find' could have been buried there by Walter Bagnall.

Was it he only treasures Bagnall and Peverly buried? Is more to be found?

Outer Heron Island

This island lies just a few miles offshore from Boothbay Harbor.

Around 1900, two young men came to Outer Heron Island from New York. They had a map of the island showing where a chest of pirate gold was supposedly buried.

The two never revealed how this map came into their possession. With a specially constructed auger that could be lengthened indefinitely by adding sections of iron rod, they started boring near a lone, grotesquely shaped spruce tree at the highest point of the island.

Pirate's Map?

After a month of constant work, and at a depth of 30 feet, the auger brought up oaken chips. They penetrated this, and the bit came up with particles of what seemed to be gold.

The two then hired two Italian laborers and excavated a 30-foot shaft. At this depth, a 6-foot oak plank was found, and that was all. The gold had come from a copper spike which the auger point had scraped.

The mystery is how did a copper spike and a six-foot plank get 30 feet underground, unless some kind of excavating had been done years before? No report of any treasures being found in the area can be located.

Stories of treasure buried by Captain William Kidd are so numerous that they would fill an entire book and a lifetime to investigate them all.

Casco Bay Island Treasures

The many islands of Casco Bay represent an excellent opportunity to secret treasure. Pirates could hide treasure on these isolated islands with little fear of it being found before they could return and collect it on their return trip to England and Europe from whence they came..

Jewell Island

Captain Kidd Treasure

Captain Kidd, fearing imminent capture, is said to have put ashore and buried his treasure on Jewell Island off Portland Head. He then marked the spot with either a square flat rock or reversed compass carved on a tree. He is reported to have made a map for finding his hoard of gold and jewels. The map has not been found.

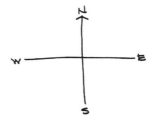

Beach at the Punch Bowl on Jewell Island

A second pirate and smuggler, Captain Chase, is part of Jewell Island pirate lore. It is said that Chase would post lanterns to lure innocent ships unfamiliar with Maine's waters onto the rocky shore. Chase and his men would then plunder the wreck scooping up anything of value and murdering any surviving crew.

Whether Kidd ever visited the island is unknown, but there is a story, backed up by considerable evidence, that a Captain Jonathan Chase found a large treasure on the island, killing his helper and burying him during the recovery. No record of what happened to Chase or the money can be found.

Jewell Island can be reached by private boat or water taxi including the Portland Express Water Taxi, Atlantic Water Taxi and Casco Bay Water Taxi . Are you ready to find pirate treasure in the woods or sand?

Bailey Island Treasure

On Bailey Island there is a well-authenticated story of pirate treasure actually having been found. In 1850 a farmer named John Wilson was duck hunting on the island when, in an attempt to retrieve a fallen bird, he slipped into a crevice between two ledges.

Pirate treasure in the rocks

In his scramble to climb out, he uncovered an iron pot filled with pieces of Spanish gold. He exchanged these for $12,000 in coin of the realm, a comfortable fortune at that time.

Is this the only treasure hidden on the island or is this find only a portion of a much larger cache?

Pond Island

Pond Island Light

Pond Island is a small island found yards off of Popham Beach and Popham Beach State Park and Fort Baldwin. Pond Island is a National Wildlife refuge and visitation may be limited. The beach and fort however, represent a fantastic treasure hunting opportunity.

Early in the 18th century it is reported that a conscripted sailor escaped from the pirate Captain Lowe's ship "Don Pedro." The ship was carrying a load of jewelry, gold and silver from Mexico to Spain. Somewhere off the coast of New York a British frigate spotted the pirate's ship. The British chased them all the way to Casco Bay where they lost them in a dense fog.

The pirates came ashore on Pond Island and are said to have buried their treasure on the island planning to return for it once they were free of the pursuing frigate. The loot, reportedly worth $100,000 in the 1700s, must be worth multi millions today.

Lowe never returned to recover the loot, and was executed by a French court for piracy.

A pot of gold coins was found by a farmer on Pond Island so Edward Lowe or other pirates may have hidden treasure on this island.

Cliff Island

The Island, located at the outer edge of Casco Bay, was once the home of a nefarious "Moon Cusserrs" known as Captain Keiff. The way of Moon Cusserrs was to lure unsuspecting ships onto the rocky shores on moonless nights.

Moon Cusserrs luring a ship ashore

He would tie a lantern to a pole and display it along the most dangerous part of the shoreline. Ships at sea would be misguided by this false navigational light and be wrecked on the reefs and ledges of the island. Keiff would kill any survivors of the wrecks, and then salvage the cargo.

In those days, while it wasn't encouraged, illegal salvaging was condoned, and no questions were asked when someone sold salvaged goods. Keiff is supposed to have made a fortune in his bloodthirsty occupation.

There is a place on the island still known as Keiff's Gardens. He lived alone in the log hut he built at this spot and where legend reports he dragged and buried his victims. Local stories say that somewhere on the island a large part of Keiff's money is still buried; probably not far from the graves of the seamen he murdered.

Haskell Island

Harpswell Neck - Is reported to be one of several places along the Maine coast that Captain Kidd and several other pirates are said to have hidden their treasure.

According to the "Folklore of Maine" in the Library of the Maine Historical Society, one of the Haskell brothers took ill and the other rowed to the mainland to get medical help.

While he was gone a band of bounty hunters came to the island and found what was said to be part of Captain Kidd's treasure but were discovered by the ailing Haskell brother.

To keep their secret the bounty hunters killed and slashed the Haskell brother to pieces in an attempt to make it look as though the island's many cats had done the gruesome deed.

Did the bounty hunters find all of the hidden treasure; or is

Murderous pirate on Haskell Island

there yet more to be discovered.

Orrs Island

The story is that while Captain Kit was plowing his field he struck what reports described as a "pot of gold." He and his eleven children lived the good life thereafter.

Elm Island

In 1840 John Wilson made a meager living doing odd jobs, hunting & fishing. One day he took his old row boat over to Elm Island to do some bird hunting. While eating his lunch, a great shot presented itself; he took aim & fired.

He only wounded the bird, which scurried away with Wilson in hot pursuit. He hadn't run very far when the ground below him gave way and he fell into a hole. Stunned, and with his quarry getting away he grabbed the sides of the hole for leverage to get out.

He grabbed hold of what he thought was a branch. To his great surprise the branch turned out to be the handle of a big kettle. A

1840 Bird hunter

kettle filled with gold coins worth $12K or $500K today!

John returned to his humble home and shortly thereafter bought a sizeable farm on which he lived the rest of his life in comfort.

Great Chebeague Island

The island is reached by ferry from Falmouth to Portland and is the second-largest island in Casco Bay.

Finding pirate's treasure?

In the 1860s, an old sailor who was believed to have been a pirate in his younger years and one of a pirate crew which many years before had buried a great treasure on the island.

The story has him digging in a secluded part of the island when a young island lad offered to assist him. When the offer was curtly refused, the boy leaped over the rope with which the old man had enclosed the spot where he was digging; whereupon the treasure seeking old man, in a voice quaking with anger, cried, *"I call on God and you people to witness that within a year this young fool will be tied in knots, even as I could tie this rope"*.

No one remembers now whether any treasure was found, but a short time later, the young man was soaked while fishing. He was confined to his bed with an agonizing malady, which drew up his arms and legs as if tied in knots, and when he died, soon afterward, it was necessary to break the bones of his limbs in order to get his body into the casket.

Was the old pirate retrieving the pirate treasure or is the gold still there somewhere on the island?

John's Island

One might wonder if there is any truth to the story of treasure on Johns Island, in Casco Bay. Many stories cling to this little island, which is famed as being the summer home of the Lauder family and Gene Tunney. Tradition has it that there was a large frame tavern on the north end of the island, a hangout for seamen.

One of these was a Portuguese who never did any work, but always had plenty of gold and silver to spend when he appeared from parts unknown.

This went on for years. Finally, he died in a foreign land, but before

Old well near the tavern

he breathed his last, he gave a friend a map of Johns Island, showing the location of a hidden well near the tavern.

At the bottom of the well, he said, gold and silver would be found because I helped put it there from the pirate craft *Dare Devil*, commanded by Dixie Bull. Searches have been made for this well, but without success.

Cedar Ledges

East of Ram Island in Casco Bay, three kettles of gold coins were found on Thanksgiving Day, 1852, and more might still be there.

Swan's Island, located in the Kennebec River. Is reported to be the site of another pirate cache.

Treasure in Penobscot Bay

Deer Isle

Was the New York Astor family's fortune actually founded upon the Pirate Captain William Kidd's treasure found in an iron box (with the initials WK chiseled on the lid) hidden on the property of Mr. Frederick Law Olmsted. Olmstead was a famous landscape architect and

Capt Kidd passes note

designer of New York's *Central Park* and Boston's *"Emerald Necklace."* Is there more treasure to be found on Deer Isle?

Just before Captain Kidd was to be hanged in 1710 and, after a whispered conference with his wife, Kidd was seen handing a small piece of past board her. This card bore the mysterious figures "44106818." Could the numbers indicate the longitude 4410 and latitude 6818 and the exact location of the remainder of Captain Kidd's treasure? The latitude for Deer Isle is exactly 4410! Plus, a cave on the Olmsted estate's latitude 6813, very close to the 6818 scribbled on Captain Kidd's final writing before he was hung.

Monroe Island

Located off of Owl's Point State Park in Penobscot Bay. For many years pirates and thieves reportedly used this island. Treasures are reportedly been hidden all over the island.

Oak Island

The island is located in Penobscot Bay. According to the book "Folklore of Maine," an elderly blind man is reported to have experienced a dream where a barrel of gold rolled out of a cave on a cliff into a pond below.

His description matched that of a place on Oak Island where a pond lay below a cliff with a cave. The pond was dragged for a week but the gold filled barrel was not found. There are those who still believe that gold is still waiting to be found.

Underwater barrel

Great Duck Island

This 237-acre island is located at sea approximately 10 miles south of Mt Desert Island. The northeast end of the island consists of cliffs and ledges, but fortunately contains a stony beach that provides an "all-weather" landing spot.

William Bigenho, who purchased the island in 1951, had identified it as the island on a 16th or 17th century "treasure map." His daughter later reported that her parents discovered a treasure consisting of gold, silver, and various artifacts. They were lead to the site of the treasure by a combination of the map and various signs carved on rocks, perhaps including a reversed compass.

Vinalhaven

Sunken Treasure aboard Circus Ship

For those interested in sunken treasure, somewhere in Penobscot Bay, Maine, not far from Vinalhaven, are the charred remains of the 164-foot side-wheeler *Royal Tar*, and her treasure chest of $35,000 in gold and silver.

The Royal Tar in her last moments

This is the story of a vessel that caught fire east of Fox Island in Penobscot Bay and later drifted off and sank. The ship carried 85 passengers and a menagerie of circus animals, 32 persons and all of the animals perished. The ship left St. John, New Brunswick and was headed toward Portland, ME in the year 1886.

A circus, returning to the States after a highly successful summer tour of New Brunswick, chartered the *Royal Tar* for the voyage home. The circus was almost too big to fit on the ship. Several of the *Royal Tars* lifeboats were removed in order to fit the troupe aboard.

The ship sailed for Portland, Maine, on October 21, 1836, riding very low in the water, her decks crowded with circus animals, including a gigantic Indian elephant.

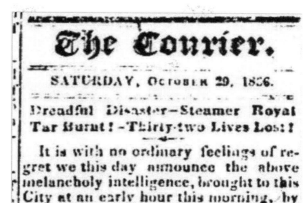

As the steamer lay at anchor about two miles off the Fox Island thoroughfare in Penobscot Bay, the ship burst into flames. The fire grew with lightning speed and soon was beyond control and the captain ordered the few lifeboats filled and lowered.

Seven hours after the fire had begun; the *Royal Tar* sank beneath the waves. It is estimated that, in the meantime, she had drifted some 20 miles, as the captain had pulled the anchor.

The $35,000 in the pursers safe was untouched by anyone during the fire. It is understandable that all concerned had to abandon the ship too hastily to think about saving the money. At least, this was the report of all those questioned following the disaster.

So the treasure was still on board the *Royal Tar* when she sank, and the facts seem to indicate that it is still there, on the bottom of Penobscot Bay with an estimated value, in today's dollars, of $3,500,000.

Finding Treasure on Maine's Mainland

Mainland Treasures

Many gold and silver coins have been discovered buried in the ground all over the state of Maine, mostly by farmers and gardeners.

There were no banks or other institutional places for the safe keeping of valuables. Therefore, folks would bury their cash and other valuables to keep them safe.

Naturally few would disclose the location of their stashes to friends or even family so, when accidental and sudden death or debilitating sickness struck, the treasure remained buried and its location unknown.

Reports of such treasure being accidentally uncovered are often kept secret and not divulged. A few reports of buried treasure finds are chronicled here.

Pot of Gold

Treasure in the Bucksport area

The Narrows - Jean Vincent de lAbadie, Baron de St. Castine, was a French nobleman who inherited land on Penobscot Bay in what is now the state of Maine. He took possession in 1665 and ran a successful trading post at the village of Pentagoet for nearly 25 years, amassing a fortune.

In 1840, Captain Stephen Grindle and his son Samuel were hauling logs to the Narrows, (an area near Bucksport) about six miles from the village, when they found a coin, a French crown. The pair dug until dark, recovering 20 more coins. It was in late November, and during the night a severe blizzard struck, so digging was suspended until the spring of 1841.

Gold coin of the era

Returning in the spring, the Grindles dug up nearly 500 coins from France, Spain, South America, Portugal, Holland, England, and Massachusetts. Was this the de Castine hoard, missing for 137 years?

The collection also contained 150 Pine Tree shillings and sixpence dated 1652. This was the first coinage struck in the colonies. The Pine Tree shillings are valued up to $2,000 each.

Records show Baron de St. Castine fled with six money chests. Thus far, only one has reportedly been found. Records further indicate that a year before the Barons flight, a French visitor had estimated the treasure to be worth $200,000. Over three hundred years have passed. How many millions are those five missing chests worth today?

Verona Island's Gold Mine

There is a real gold mine on Verona Island. The "Mispickle Mine" actually is not the cave like mine we usually think of as a gold mine but rather a shaft or hole drilled into the ground.

Mispickle is a word of German origin referring to the iron arsenic sulfide Arsenopyrite that is often associated with significant amounts of gold.

Gold mining at the "mine" was suspended in the 1940's and converted to mining of the arsenic for use in producing ammunition in support of the war effort.

Arsenopyrite

If you visit Fort Knox, just over the "Narrows Bridge" from Verona Island and overlooking the town of Bucksport, look at the indigenous stones there.

Some will be very dark and heavier than usual stones and may have lighter colored veins in them.

Don't use them to ring your campfire, as they have been known to "explode." My wife still bears the scars from our "exploding" Verona Island shore side campfire years ago.

Verona Island's Gold Mine

American Colonialist battle Great Britain off Sandy Neck and Verona Island at the mouth of the Penobscot River in 1779. America's first naval defeat occurred here and the remains of more that forty ship are scattered up the Penobscot as far as the Bangor Dam.

You probably will not find treasure but instead a piece of American history and the fledgling nation's little known naval defeat.

Some of the 43 Colonial America's ships lost in the Battle known as the *Penobscot Expedition* have been found. The Penobscot River between Bangor and Brewer has at least nine sites with ships involved in the Penobscot Expedition.

Map showing the location ships scuttled in 1779

The Maine Historic Preservation Commission declares; "We've narrowed it down to 27 [sites] in the Penobscot River". Not all of the ships identity has been established.

The New Hampshire privateer *Hampden* and the ship *Hunter*, one of the largest and best of the Massachusetts privateers, were captured by the British.

The Ships and where they were lost

Active, Brigantine – Privateer 30 Guns, 16 six pounders, 14 four pounders – near Kenduskeag Stream, Bangor

Black Prince – Ship, Massachusetts Privateer – *Guns, 20-6 pounders* - near Bangor/Brewer

Defence, Brig – Privateer – Devereaux Cove in Stockton Springs

Charming Sally, Ship Massachusetts Privateer Guns, 20 9-pounders - near Bangor/Brewer

Diligent Brig – Guns, 14 – 4 pounders – near Bangor/Brewer The *Diligent* was formerly the British warship HMB *Diligent.* She was captured off Sandy Hook, NJ in May of 1779 by the Continental Sloop *Providence.*

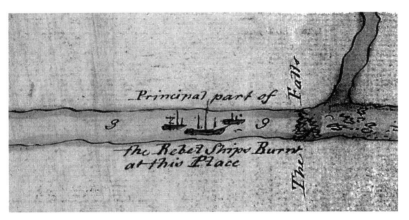

Map showing the location of burned ships below the Bangor Dam

Hazard, Brig – Massachusetts State Navy. Guns, 18 6 – Pounders - near Bangor/Brewer

Hector, Ship – Massachusetts Privateer, Guns – 20-9 pounders - near Bangor/Brewer

Monmouth, Ship – Massachusetts Privateer, Guns, 20– 6 pounders – near Bangor/Brewer

Pidgeon. Sloop – unarmed Transport - near Bangor/Brewer

Providence –Sloop of War – *Guns, 14-6 pounders* –She was the first vessel authorized for use by the Continental Navy (1775) and fired the first shot of the American Revolution.   Providence was the first command of Col. John Paul Jones of "The British are coming" fame. near Bangor/Brewer

Putnam, Brig – Privateer - Penobscot River

Revenge, Sloop or Brig - Penobscot River

Sally, unknown Privateer - Penobscot River

Samuel. - Winterport

Spring Bird, Paul Revere's Ship - Frankfort

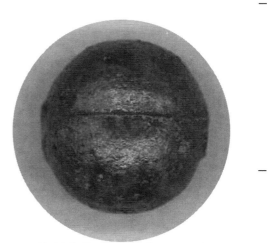

Sky Rocket, Brig Privateer, burned off Verona

A transport - mouth of the Sedgeunkedunk Stream in South Brewer

British Grape Shot from 1779 Penobscot Expedition Battle

Tiranicide, Brig – Massachusetts State Navy – Guns, 20-6 pounders, near Bangor/Brewer

Vengence, Brig – Privateer - Penobscot River

Warren – Winterport

Macias Region

Frequented by Several Pirate

Captain Rhodes

If you are ever in the areas of the coastal town of
Machias, you will hear tales of loot hidden by the
notorious pirate, Captain Rhodes. He roamed this
shore in 1675, using the sheltered inlet of the Machias
River as a hideout and a place for careening his ship.

Captains Harry Thompson and Starbird

Another Machias area treasure is also stashed along
Starbirds Creek. Years ago, Captain Harry Thompson
and another buccaneer named Starbird frequently

used the entrance
to the Machias
River as a
rendezvous
between voyages.
As a consequence,
they used a nearby
creek, named for
Starbird, to cache
their plunder.
Thompson was said
to have marked

Is this buried pirate treasure?

some trees and to have drawn a crude map to aid his
children in locating this trove, but they apparently
misinterpreted the clues, for they dug without success.

The Brothers Flynn

In the same general area, Brothers Island, named for
two brothers called Flynn, is reputedly a hiding place
for their trove. However, information concerning this
cache is not easy to establish.

Pirates Samuel Bellamy and Paulsgrave Williams

Bellamy's Jolly Roger

There reportedly is a hidden underground vault containing pirate treasure in the vicinity of the Machias River. Legend says that the Pirate, Black Bellamy built the vault beneath his wooden fort on the river. The fort is now gone, but it was known to be located near the bridge on State route A1.

Other version reports the treasure mouth of the Machias River is not where the two pirates had their stronghold, but further upriver. They did dig a subterranean treasure house, but it was not inside the fort. There is little doubt but that the vault holds a large hoard of what we call treasure today.

After looting a number of ships, the pirates arrived at a destination selected by Captain Bellamy, the only navigator on board. The spot was near the mouth of the Machias River, far from any civilized community at that time. It was here that Bellamy and Williams put their plan into action. The cargo had to be hidden very well before they sailed to continue their pirating.

A large vault was excavated to serve as a treasure house and their treasure secreted. When all of this was done, and the *Whydah* had been overhauled, Bellamy and Williams set sail again. After several forays, the treasure house was filled.

The headquarters of Bellamy and Williams, near the mouth of the Machias River, has disappeared. But somewhere nearby is hidden one of the richest pirate caches in North America, one that has never been reported found.

Allagash Region

Lost Smuggling Fortune

A story treasure on the Allagash River is that of Anse Hanley. During the early days of timber cutting, the lumber companies were constantly in trouble with squatters. These people would carve out a small homestead on company land, then hint to the owners that if they were forced to move, a forest fire might start that would destroy millions of dollars worth of timber. In most cases, the squatters stayed on the property.

One such land parasite was Anse Hanley. Around 1900, Hanley came to Fort Kent, accompanied by his wife and two children.

Whiskey Still Diagram

After obtaining supplies, he moved up the Allagash River in Aroostook County, where he squatted. During the next few years, Hanley engaged in making whiskey for sale to the loggers.

It was said of his homemade product, if a man can drink it and come back for more, he would live forever. Hanley also sold farm products and engaged in smuggling whiskey, guns, and cigarettes from Canada, which he sold to American sportsmen and hunters. When Hanley died, he left a rumored $60,000, some of which he had hidden before his death, and it has never be found.

80

Portland Area

Portland

An influential politician's gardener digs up a 1579 silver sixpence at the State Street address.

A vacant lot at the corners of Vaughan and Brackett streets in Portland yields a 1655 "Leg Dollar." It was so named because of the one legged military figure shown on the face of the coin.

Saco

William Edgecomb was working in his garden on the Ferry Road in Saco in the spring of 1931 when he dug up a gold coin dated 1723.

Biddeford

In the summer of 1931 two gardeners while transplanting flowers discovered 63 Spanish gold and silver coins scattered around in the dirt.

The Biddeford Journal described one of the coins: "Elie T. Labbe took one of the coins in a splendid state of preservation bearing the date 1805 to a local bank this

Spanish coin of Charles IV 1805

morning where he was told that it was a $1 Spanish coin of the reign of Charles IV of Spain. He was also informed that the value of the coin at this time is $65."

Labbe told the Journal reporter that he intended to do some more digging before totaling up his buried treasure, but he didn't believe it would ever amount to enough for him to be able to retire from the florist business.

He also made a plea for help from local historians in solving the mystery of how Spanish coins might have come to be buried on his land at 200 Pool St.,

Biddeford Pool

The town was attacked by the British man-of-war *Bulwark* on June 16, 1814. The *Harmoine*, *Catherine* and *Equator* were sunk. One ship in the stocks (unknown name) was burned and one ship the *Victory* was stolen for ransom of $6000.

"Family Silver" buried at Biddeford Pool?

John Staples Locke wrote of the incident in his 1880 book, "Shores of Saco Bay." *"Messengers were dispatched through the country on horseback, to alarm the inhabitants. All the men capable of bearing arms left their fields and hastened towards the Pool. Women and children fled to the woods with their valuables. One aged lady tells of taking the silver of a wealthy Saco family and burying it in the woods near where is now the Abenakee Golf Club."*

Open land still exists around the golf course, along the shore and out to East Point.

Egyptian Mummies

Portland - There is an unusual treasure that is probably still where it was stored, about ten miles southwest of Portland waiting to be found.

To some people the idea of searching for Egyptian mummies might seem sacrilegious, but remember that the mummies have already been taken from their original graves, transported to the United States, and are worth, on today's collectors market, in excess of $50,000 each. Here is the story.

In 1857, and thereafter for several years, newspaper publishers in this country faced a severe shortage of rags, which were necessary to add strength and body to wood fibers used in paper sheets. As the shortage of rags increased, large numbers of small newspapers went out of business.

Augustus Stanwood, a printer in Portland, Maine, was greatly affected by this rag shortage. Realizing that he would go broke, Stanwood looked around for a much-needed source of this ever-increasing shortage of fiber.

One night, while drinking with a sea captain, Stanwood told him of his troubles. The sailing captain suggested using the cloth wrappings of mummies. (At this time the Egyptian gravesites were being exploited, and thousands, throughout the world, were selling artifacts, coffins, and mummies.)

Mummy

Augustus made a deal with the ship's captain to obtain several dozen of these cloth-wrapped bodies. When the shipment arrived, Stanwood stored them on his property, in pits to preserve them, about ten miles southwest of Portland.

During the next three to seven years, he used about half of the mummies, putting their linen and cotton wrappings into his paper grinders. The pulp made a very good grade of paper stock.

About this time the rag shortage let up because of the Civil War and the capture of huge stores of cotton by Union forces throughout the South. Thus, Stanwood did not need to use the rest of his mummies. After he tried to sell them and couldn't, Stanwood left the mummies in the pits he had dug on his property.

After Stanwood died, few people even remembered the mummies, and they are, as far as can be determined, still buried on the old Stanwood property, about ten miles southwest of Portland, Maine. If you aren't afraid of ghosts, this unusual treasure could be worth thousands of dollars today.

Paper Making

84

More Lost Treasures

Manchester - One of Maine's little-known treasures concerns Jim Dolliver, a wealthy sawmill owner who secreted over $1,000,000 in gold for safekeeping near The Forks, now Manchester in the 1890s. He had previously made an overland journey to Montreal, where had converted his notes, checks, shares, and bonds into gold sovereigns. He liked the feel of gold rather than paper.

During his journey home on the old French trail, Dolliver noticed some men following him. Were they robbers? Would they kill him? As Jim tore through the dense woods to evade the real, or imagined, robbers, he went completely insane from fear. He is said to have buried his money in an old stump.

1858 gold sovereigns

Relatives later stated that Dolliver died battling imaginary thieves. These same relatives offered three-quarters of the money to whomever should find it, and they spent $3,000 in efforts to discover its where-abouts, to no avail. As far as is known, this cache has never been found.

85

Moved into Cave to Avoid Neighbors

Liberty - This little town in Waldo County, also boasts of a lost treasure of $70,000 in gold coins. This trove belonged to Timothy Barrett, who lived there in the early 1700s.

Folks noticed that Barrett always seemed to have an inexhaustible supply of money, although he never worked. Was he a retired pirate?

That explanation seemed to satisfy his neighbors. In time, the old fellow became vexed with people always asking him about the source of his wealth, so he moved across nearby George's Stream and dug a cave for a home. He cultivated a small garden for his simple needs.

Cave in the woods

When old Barrett finally died, villagers began a great search for his fortune. A couple of fellows dug up an iron kettle near the cave. It was filled with ancient French coins. However, this was believed to have been only a small part of the main cache, which is still safe in the ground near George's Stream.

Benedict Arnold's Gold

Stratton – October 19, 1775 - Benedict Arnold and his troops passed through the area on their way up the North Branch of the Dead River to fight in the ill-fated Battle of Quebec.

On their way, a canoe carrying a chest full of gold

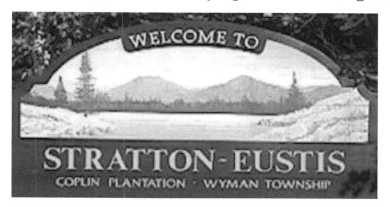

coins went over a falls and capsized throwing the chest into the foaming river.

Not even contemporaries of Benedict Arnold knew how much was in the lost chest of gold. Supposedly lost beneath one of the falls of the River, on the abortive march against the walls of Quebec, the loot has never been found.

During Arnold's famous court martial in Philadelphia, he was asked to account for the money, and while the one-day traitor did produce sketchy records accounting for $5,000, the remainder was lost in the forest wilderness of Maine, or so he claimed.

While no one is certain, the chest and the gold are supposed to be somewhere north of the modern village of Stratton on the Dead River.

Finding
Maine's
Gemstones,
Silver and
Gold

Where to Find Gemstones

Maine is home gemstones such as tourmalines, beryl, amethyst, garnet, and topaz. At least one mineral, beryllonite, has been found *nowhere outside Maine*, and this state has yielded the finest emerald beryl ever found in the United States. In mineral production, Maine stands about midway among the states, with the annual yield being valued at about $6,000,000. One-third of the state is still unexplored in respect to mineral

Tourmaline, from Newry, Maine mine

resources, and only limited areas have received adequate investigation.

Mineral & Gem Collecting Places

Mining Locations
There are several mining locations between Bethel and South Paris:

- Bethel Outdoor Adventure,
- Songo Pond,
- Western Maine Mineral,
- Creaser Jewelers,
- Perham's of West Paris, and
- Kings' Hill Inn.

These mining locations may be the best bet for finding gems such as tourmaline, quartz, rose quartz, and crystal. Mining locations in the Bethel area are centered on Mt. Mica. Workshops are provided by Bethel Outdoor Adventure or Western Maine Mineral, mineral. A hammer, shovel, pan, and chisel are helpful tools when sorting through rocks.

Several other mining locations are scattered throughout Maine including Coos Canyon Rock and Gift, Hermit Island, Grafton Notch State Park, Auburn Recreation Parks Department, and the Desert of Maine. Coos Canyon, located on the Swift River in Byron, ME has some gold pockets scattered throughout the river, but is more a swimming and camping site than a mining hot spot.

Hermit Island has a similar appeal, but is located on the ocean instead of a river. Hermit Island holds some promise of crystal discoveries and mica scatters the beaches at low tide. Both Coos Canyon and Hermit Island are relaxing locations that are perfect for those looking to camp for a weekend near water and possibly find some gold or gems.

Mt. Appetite in Auburn, ME is home to several types of crystals, including green and pink tourmaline, and transparent smoky quartz.

Where Silver Has Been Found

Silver is found in most of the lead and zinc localities, and the copper ores at Bluehill. That there are considerable bodies of lead and zinc of definite value has been known since they were first mined in 1860. Some pure silver has been mined at Sullivan and elsewhere.

More specific locations of different mineral sites can be obtained from the State Geology Department at Augusta, Maine.

Lost Silver Mine

The legend states that Indians under a Captain Sunday mined silver near the town of Cornish, Cumberland County. The place was marked by three small hills flanking the Saco River near its junction with the Ossipee River. The mined silver was stored and never used.

After working the mine for several years, the Indians sold the land on which it was located to William Phillips, who spent the remainder of his life searching for the mine, but never found it.

Boston – Acton Silver Mines

Acton is a small town in Southern Maine, York County, situated along the New Hampshire border. Silver was discovered in 1877, followed by a decade of mining and prospecting, after which the mines were abandoned. The town lies northwest of Sanford on Route 109, which continues into New Hampshire.

There are several mines on various properties. Inquire locally. A compass and insect repellent (May-Sept.) may be useful here. Watch out for vertical mine shafts.

Directions:

Driving: From Sanford, take U.S. Rte. 202 south to blinking light in East Lebanon. Turn right and go north 2.55 miles (keeping to right and then to left as you pass through North Lebanon). Turn right onto Will Goding Road and continue north 2.50 miles (pavement ends at 1.10 miles). Park at head of trail on right side of road.

Walking: Follow trail north 1,400 feet to fork. Take trail to right and continue about 100 feet to old bridge with beaver dam and pond on left. This is head of Little River. Proceed on faint trail (which will turn north) 900 feet to old mine and shaft on left. Alternatively, from old bridge walk south along east bank of Little River (no trail) for about 450 feet to the Boston-Acton and other mines.

Silver from Maine Mine

93

Where to Find Gold in Maine

Coos Canyon

Maine is a very big state, and anyone who has driven around there knows just how huge it is. Lots and lots of trees (and moose of course)! But, there is also lots of gold to be found in Maine.

Coos Canyon, Byron, ME

By far the most popular spot is in Byron at Coos Canyon along the Swift River and the East Branch of the Swift River. There is a Rock & Mineral shop there called Coos Canyon Rock & Gift. You can buy prospecting supplies there as well as learn panning techniques.

Coos Canyon is a scenic, rocky gorge carved through bedrock by the Swift River. The Swift River is one of more than a half dozen streams and rivers in Maine known to harbor deposits of gold. According to the Maine Department of Conservation's Gold Fact Sheet, "Gold occurs in several geologic environments in Maine: in bedrock, in sediments that were eroded from bedrock by glaciers, and in stream deposits derived from either of these sources."

Location: Coos Canyon is located in the town of Byron, Maine, on Route 17. It will come up on your right as you're headed toward Rangeley on Route 17 West.

Admission: There is free parking available at the Coos Canyon site.

Pan for Gold: Bring your own panning equipment, or rent gear and take a quick lesson in panning at the Coos Canyon Rock & Gift Shop located, across Route 17 from Coos Canyon.

Mother Lode of Gold in Southern Maine

Somewhere in the middle of southwestern Maine, in Oxford County, there exists a mother lode of gold beyond the wildest dreams of any treasure hunter.

Pure conjecture? Not at all; that statement is based on solid fact and research.

Entrance to a Mine

For 50 years, concentrated efforts have been made by professional geologists to find the source of gold in Oxford County's brooks, lakes, and ponds. The precious metal is found everywhere, and platinum is found occasionally. At the present time, research is continuing in the Wilson Mills area, very close to the New Hampshire border. There is very definitely gold in them thar hills, particularly in the region of Eustis.

Swift River Gold

Near **Byron,** the Swift River and its many feeders have produced more gold than all of the other Maine regions combined. Anyone who can handle a pan will find small traces of the color if he is willing to spend the time. As many as a dozen persons can be seen panning the stream on any given day. A few do their prospecting by searching behind the stream on any given day. A few do their prospecting by searching behind the upturned stones and boulders where small nuggets sometimes collect.

Trappers have been finding a small amount of gold in the Swift River almost since the area was first opened to settlement. Within recent memory, over $7,000 of the yellow stuff was taken from among a jumbled pile of rocks at a bend in the river. Perley Whitney took several thousand dollars worth over a period of years from one of the branches. Two Boston vacationers panned almost $5,000 in two weeks time from one of the small brooks that flow into the Swift River.

Rangeley Area Gold and Platinum

Northwest of Byron is the Rangeley lake chain, a

Gold found in streams like this one

popular vacation area in the northeast. In Nile Brook, not far from the village of Rangeley, both platinum and gold have been found. All of the streams flowing into the chain of lakes contain the precious metal, and in a few a numbers of freshwater pearls have been found.

But it is the area extending from the village of Eustis southward to Lake Parmachenne that causes the excitement among those who search for gold.

It is generally believed that the mother lode is somewhere in this general area. Kibbey Brook, which flows past the village, has produced some outstanding crystals, as has the Magalloway River, southwest of the town. Trappers often find traces of gold while running their lines.

Panning for gold for fun and Profit in Maine

Remember that you're in a region that even prominent scientists believe harbors a fabulous mother lode. There is nothing mythological about the gold of Maine.

The following counties in Maine have each produced some gold: Aroostook, Cumberland, Franklin, Hancock, Kennebec, Knox, Oxford, Penobscot, Somerset, Waldo, and Washington.

There are certainly more areas that likely have gold bearing gravels, and a bit of research will increase your chances of prospecting success.

More Places to Find Gold

Here are some other locations as listed by the state of Maine:

River	Town	County
Swift River and its tributaries	Byron area	Oxford, Franklin
Sandy River	Madrid to New Sharon	Franklin
South Branch-Penobscot River	Sandy Bay; Bald Mtn; Prentiss	Somerset
Gold Brook	Bowman	Oxford
Gold Brook	Chain of Ponds; Kibby	Franklin
Gold Brook	Chase Stream	Somerset
Gold Brook	T5 R6; Appleton Township	Somerset
Nile Brook	Dallas; Rangeley	Franklin
Kibby Stream	Kibby	Franklin
St. Croix River	Baileyville	Washington

Finding Treasure in

New Hampshire

and the

Isles of Shoals

New Hampshire

Nashua - During the French Revolution, King Louis XV commissioned the crown's jewelers to create a most exquisite necklace for his mistress Madam DuBarry at a cost of 80,000 pounds; the equivalent of many millions today.

Before the necklace could be completed the king died leaving the craftsmen without a customer. They attempted to interest the Queen, Marie Antoinette, in the necklace but she considered it gaudy and hideous and wanted nothing to do with it.

Diamond necklace commissioned by King Louii XV

Countess Jeanne de la Motte, an enemy of Marie, after learning of the necklace recognized the opportunity to gain revenge upon the Queen whom she despised.

She convinced Cardinal of France, Cardinal Rohan, that Marie Antoinette was infatuated with him and led the unsuspecting Cardinal to believe that if he gave Marie Antoinette the necklace, he could have her undying affection.

The complicated plot thickens; he commissions the conniving Countess to buy the necklace (using his money), which she did. The necklace then mysteriously disappears and she spreads the rumor that Antoinette and the Cardinal were having and affair.

The jewelers demand payment from Antoinette and of course she knows nothing of what they speak. The countess's plot unravels and she is sent to prison. The revolution became bloody and Marie lost her head on Oct 16 1793. The diamond necklace was never found.

The story continues. According to attorney James Sullivan of Nashua, NH, an agent of the Countess fled to England with the necklace and then traveled with the necklace to Montreal, Canada.

There he hired an Indian guide and traveled south to settle on Pennichuck Island near Nashua, NH. He planned to settle there until the turmoil of the French Revolution and Antoinette's missing jewels subsided.

His plan to sell the jewels in New York for a fortune fell apart when he suddenly became ill and died. Before he died however, he told his Indian guide where he had buried a "wampum belt full of bright stones." "Buried three and a half feet underground at the northwest corner of the Island with four stones marking the spot."

Shortly after the French Revolution ended in 1795, two French officers arrived at Nashua, NH. They had tracked the countess's agent with the necklace to Pennichuck Island. They searched the entire island and founding nothing and returned discouraged and empty handed to France.

In 1912 Randolph Farley, a descendant of the island owner, perpetuated the legend of the diamonds by addendum to the deed of the property which he sold to the Proctor Brothers Co. It reads: "I and my heirs and assigns relinquish to the said Proctor Bros, all claim to any Treasure buried on the Pennichuck Island by an Englishman and his Indian Guide In 1785 consisting of Diamonds and Gold."

Might your dowsing skills help you find the missing diamonds?

The Silver Madonna

Near Conway - On September 13, 1759 Lord Jeffrey Amherst ordered Major Robert Rodgers to attack and destroy the Indian town of St. Francis in Canada, which for fifty years had launched raiding parties in New England. That same night Rodgers set out with two hundred of his hand picked New England Rangers. They arrived on October 5 at a very auspicious moment. The Abenaki Indians, who composed seventy-five percent of the population of St. Francis, were celebrating a wedding.

Silver Statue of Madonna

The Rangers struck at dawn and caught the Indians completely by surprise. Wigwams and cabins were set afire, and the accurate fire of expert marksmen mowed down the startled Indians as they emerged. Some of the Indians fled into the mission church of St. Francois de Sales, but the New Englanders, enraged at the number of scalps of women and children on display in the village, pursued them and killed them all in front of the altar. Father Roubaud, the Jesuit priest in charge, was shot down and the church was ransacked and set fire to. The Rangers carried off a golden chalice, two large gold candlesticks, a cross, and a large silver statute of the Madonna.

Realizing that the scattered Indian forces would soon regroup and counter attack, Rodgers ordered his men to scour the town for provisions to prepare for a forced march retreat. "Food is essential," he told them. "Fill your knapsacks with food. Carry nothing else." Unfortunately many of the Rangers concentrated on plunder, and a large supply of food was allowed to burn.

Two hours after the attack began the Rangers, along with five Indian captives and five freed prisoners, were

Church afire

marching to the south. They lost their way. Bad weather dogged them; and by the time they reached Lake Memthremagog near Newport, VT, they were starving. Rodgers broke the column up into seven units that were to separate and hunt in different directions then re-assemble at the head of the Connecticut River. Bad fortune hounded them all. Two of the units were wiped out by pursuing Indians. Fish and game could not be found. Heavy snows and bitter cold attacked them. Stragglers starved or died of exposure or, worse yet, were tortured to death by vengeful Abenakis.

Rodgers and a few men made it to the Connecticut River but were too weak to go any further. Rodgers and one companion set forth on a raft and, after incredible hardships, reached the settlements where they dispatched rescue teams upriver to save the few who survived.

One of the Ranger groups succeeded in avoiding both starvation and the pursuing Indians through the efforts of two captive squaws who foraged edible bulbs and roots and kept them from getting lost. A British captain who had been attached to the Rangers by Lord Amherst commanded this group.

At the mouth of the Connecticut one of the Rangers named Amos Parsons persuaded nine of the others to mutiny. During the night they opened the packs which still held the loots from St. Francis de Sales chapel, including the Madonna, gagged the two Indian guides, and crossed the Connecticut River heading into the White Mountains.

The next morning the younger Indian stabbed her guard in the throat and escaped into the forest. Amos Parsons wreaked vengeance on the remaining captive, forcing her to carry his heavy knapsack and beating her on the slightest pretense. If any of the ex-Rangers protested, Parsons threatened to kill them. The Indian woman led them into the Israel River region of the White Mountains where they became hopelessly lost. In spite of savage beatings, she refused to scour for food.

A blizzard struck. The squaw contrived to kill Parsons as he slept, and was herself killed by one of the Rangers. Weeks later, a lone, half-mad, starving Ranger emerged near Conway to tell a confused tale of starvation and death.

Some of the treasures taken from St. Francis de Sales were later recovered, but the lost silver Madonna is still missing. Over the years several treasure hunters are said to have died seeking it.

Near Portsmouth

Legend says Governor John Wentworth buried $25,000 in coins and silverware near Portsmouth.

He presumably hid this before fleeing to the north during the parlous times of the Revolutionary War. It is known that Wentworth was a man of considerable wealth.

Separately, the site of his summer home has been a prime archaeological focal point for many years. On the shore of a body of water that today bears his name, Lake Wentworth, various small British coins and numerous artifacts have been located.

North Littleton

Priceless treasure seized almost two centuries ago in a famed Indian Raid by Rogers' Rangers, may still lie buried in northern Vermont & New Hampshire.

White Devil

Here is one version of what occurred in that incredible raid & retreat of 1759 by the. Sherbooke Daily Record 3/20/1987

"Wabo Madahondo- the white devil", was the name given by the Abenakis of St. Francis of the Lake to Major Robert Rogers. Sir General Jeffrey Amherst ordered the latter to go on an avenging expedition against the Indians.

On the 4th or 5th of October, 1759, heading 142 colonial soldiers called the "Rangers" made an early morning attack on village of St. Francis of the Lake with incredible brutality. Three hours after they arrived, 200 men, women and children lay dead amongst the smoking ruins of their homes, their Church and the small Jesuits' Convent.

The night before the attack the Rangers discovered 600 to 700 scalps displayed on stakes as trophies for everyone to see. This surely did not attract their pity.

Scalps on display

After this raid, the Rangers carrying the loot, returned up the St. Francis River in order to reach Little Forks.

"At the "Little Forks", Rogers divided his 140 men into several small parties...and promising those who should take the old Indian Trail (by Island Pond) and down the Nulhegn that he would send them provisions and aid at the mouth of the Upper Ammonoosuc river, where, four years earlier, he had built a stockade called "Fort Wentworth."

Aid never reached Rogers or his men and, starving they reportedly buried the treasure somewhere near the mouth of Cow Brook, in North Littleton, N.H., where that stream falls into the Connecticut. The brook has changed its course several times so the treasure can be anywhere in the region.

Perhaps a bit of remote dowsing is in order.

Green Hill, Barrington

Cache of Silver Coins

The Hayes family first settled the land on the southerly side of Green Hill in Barrington. Paul Hayes was a prominent settlers of the town and one of the original founders of the Congregational Church. His son, James, known in his day as "Jeems" was the man who made Green Hill famous. For in the 1816 there was a very bad cold snap which ruined most of the crops planted that summer. Wadleigh's history of Dover records some of that summer's bad weather - "May 15, frozen hard enough on plowed ground to bear a man; June 10, heavy frost; July 11, heavy frost, killed a great deal of corn and apples; July 15, ice formed in Wason tan yard in Dover; August 20, rain and snow on the heights; August 22, heavy frost which killed corn and potatoes"

As if by a miracle Jeems Hayes had 10 acres of corn which survived all of this bad weather and produced a good crop when most other crops had failed. To obtain sufficient food people came from as far as 40 miles away to buy corn from Jeems Hayes. He charged one silver dollar per peck of corn and wouldn't accept any form of payment except for silver dollar coins. The silver dollars quickly filled a good sized trunk and Jeems soon became one of the richest men around. Mr. Hayes died soon after the famine year though and so didn't get to enjoy his newly obtained fortune for very long.

Some of the money was lent to the Strafford bank in Dover during a panic but much of it was kept in the old trunk by Jeems' widow until one night when Jeems' grandson Jim and some of his friends were having a good time getting drunk in the family house. A drunken brawl broke out over some matter or another and Jeems' widow became afraid that her money would be stolen and so she opened the trunk and took all of the silver dollars she could carry in her apron and quietly snuck out of the house.

She headed westward past the old Hayes family burying ground into the deep woods. She wandered around for a while looking for a place to bury her money. She found a spot in the middle of a triangle formed by 3 large trees where she dug a deep hole in the soft earth, put in the contents of her apron and then neatly covered it and then went back home.

A few days later she went back to retrieve her money but she couldn't locate the triangle of trees again. She summoned help from her family and neighbors but after an extensive search they gave up without ever finding the money. Many have since tried to find the treasure but no one (as of 1930) had reported it found.

Near Colebrook

Coos County, located far in the northern regions of the state and quite distant from the sea, is where some of Captain Kidd's treasure is said to have been buried, and "old coins have been found." If so, there is a remote possibility that such a cache could have or still does include Massachusetts silver coins. However, it is difficult to imagine that Captain Kidd would have spent a week or more journeying to this remote inland location after he anchored his ship on the New Hampshire coast.

Governor John Wentworth is said by some to have buried $25,000 in coins and silverware near Portsmouth, presumably before fleeing to the north during the parlous times of the Revolutionary War. It is known that Wentworth was a man of considerable wealth. Separately, the site of his summer home on the shore of the body of water that today bears his name, Lake Wentworth, in Wolfeboro, New Hampshire, has been a prime archaeological focal point for many years, various small British coins and numerous artifacts have been located there, and today a small local association supports its heritage. Despite reading several accounts, the author has never located any reliable reports of his having hidden any treasure, but anything is possible.

Isles of Shoals

Choice of Pirates for Centuries

The islands that comprise the Isle of Shoals: Star Island, Appledore Island, Smuttynose Island, White Island, Cedar Island, Duck Island, Lunging Island, Eastern Island, Shag Island , Mingo Island and Seavey Island, have been reported to have been favored by pirates since the 1600's.

Smuttynose Island, at 25 acres (10 ha), is the third-largest island. It is known as the site of Blackbeard's honeymoon, later for the shipwreck of the Spanish ship *Sagunto* in 1813,

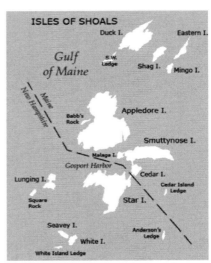

Islands are separated by Maine/NH state lines

Malaga Island is a diminutive island just to the west of Smuttynose, connected to it by a breakwater. That breakwater was built around 1820 by Captain Samuel Haley, who is reputed to have paid for its construction with proceeds from four bars of pirate silver that he found under a flat rock on the island.

The Isles of Shoals off the coast of New Hampshire and just about every landing place along NH's short (about 17 miles) seacoast have been long regarded as prime sources for hunting pirate treasure, although little has actually been reported as found there; not really surprising.

110

The Islands were a Favorite of Pirates

This offshore group includes Smuttynose Island, said to be a particularly rich possibility, for many pirates, including in particular Jack Quelch, thought this was a great location to bury silver and gold (if after a search there, a treasure seeker is in need of a libation, some Old Brown Dog Ale made by the Smuttynose Brewing Co. in nearby Portsmouth can offer succor).

Ned Low and William Fly were two other pirates who liked the area. Cotton Mather, the Massachusetts diarist and prominent justice, recorded that Fly's career was especially bloodthirsty, but lasted only 35 days before he was tried and hanged in Boston, where Fly helped the hangman tie the knot for his neck.

Appledore Island, not far away, is said to be laden with treasure just waiting to be found, although a lot of people have tried. Ditto for Star Island.

Londoner Island, later called Lunging Island, is where Blackbeard is said to have buried treasure, on the side of the island facing the Star Island Hotel across the water; Blackbeard is said to have had 14 wives and a bevy of concubines, apparently a treasure of another sort.

The lower reaches of the Piscataqua River, which empties into the Atlantic at Portsmouth, are said to be where Samuel Bellamy cached some supplies and possibly coins.

We have collected several legendary accounts of piratical activity in these islands. Many of the legends have been supported by the finds of gold and silver coins as well as silver bars.

Blackbeard's buried treasure on Smuttynose Island

Blackbeard took fourteen wives and fathered forty children. He is said to have honeymooned on Smuttynose with his thirteenth before leaving her to guard the treasure while awaiting his return. One legend reports that Blackbeard buried treasure on a halfmoon shaped beach somewhere on Smuttynose Island.

Pirates bury treasure

His treasure is reported to be consist of silver bars and pieces-of-eight. The silver bars are believed to be the ones found by a Captain Samuel Haley. Haley found five large silver bars while building a sea wall for Malaga Island. So if, indeed, those were the silver bars Blackbeard buried, then the pieces-of-eight are yet to be found.

He never did return and his bride's ghost is still occasionally seen on the island. Is she still guarding the location of the treasure or is her spirit awaiting the return of her black hearted lover?

Lunging Island

The island is the location most strongly rumored to still hold Blackbeard's buried treasure. The treasure is said to be secreted in a cave long since collapsed and covered by nearly 300 years of storm and tide. Smuttynose is also where the Spanish bark "Sagunto" sank on January, 14 1813. All hands on board died. Fourteen were found over the next few days, some having crawled ashore only to meet their maker as a frozen corpse. No treasure or cargo has ever been reported recovered.

Shipwreck on Smuttynose Yields Gold and Silver

In January 1813 a ship named *Conception* out of Cadiz, Spain, was far off its course in a storm and slid by Cedar Island and crashed ashore at Southeast Point, Smuttynose Island. Her cargo of dried fruits, almonds, bales of broadcloth, and a treasure of gold and silver went down with her crew. Considerable gold and silver was discovered shortly after the wreck on the low-tide shore. Also found was a silver pocket watch inscribed with the initials P. S.

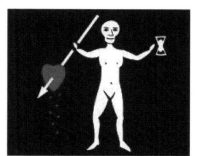

John Quelch's Pirate Flag

Pirate John Quelch Secrets Treasure on White Island White Island, which is one mile southwest of Star Island, also holds treasure buried by John Quelch and probably others at several locations on the island.

How much of Quelch's treasure is buried on the Isles of Shoals is open to conjecture. *Life Magazine*, in 1950, stated that $100,000 was buried there, about half of which has been recovered. In "1001 Lost, Buried, or Sunken Treasures", the authoritative F. L. Coffman said that Quelch's crew secreted $275,000 on Star Island and established several other caches on White Island.

Originally a pirate hunter, John Quelch turned pirate when the opportunity presented itself. In July 1703, he signed aboard the brigantine *Charles of Boston*, which was outfitted as a privateer to sail against the French in Nova Scotia and

Captain Sent Overboard

Newfoundland waters. The captain of the boat was a man named Daniel Plowman.

Captain Plowman was unhappy, however, with the caliber of the crew which was recruited to man the newly-built, eighty-ton craft. To make matters worse, he was taken ill just before the ship was set to sail.

Anthony Holding, one of the crew's ringleaders, assumed command. He locked the ailing captain in his cabin and ordered the ship out to sea. Once underway, the crew chose John Quelch to be the captain, probably because he had the most knowledge of navigation. Instead of sailing northeast to battle the French ships, the *Charles* now set a course to the south on a search for plunder in the Caribbean and the Spanish Main. Sometime after Quelch had assumed command, Captain Plowman was thrown overboard, but whether dead or alive is not known.

During the next three months Quelch made nine captures, five brigantines, a small sloop, two fishing boats, and a ship of about two hundred tons. These vessels were the property of the subjects of the King of Portugal, now an ally of the Queen of England. From these ships Quelch secured rich booty including a hundred-weight of gold dust, gold, and silver coins to the value of over one thousand pounds, ammunition, small arms, and a great quantity of fine fabrics, provisions, and rum. By attacking these ships, Quetch became a pirate, and the English Navy was on the watch for him.

Quelch arrived back at Marblehead, Massachusetts, where he was eventually arrested. However, between the time of his arrival and his arrest, he and several members of his crew managed to make their way to Star Island and White Island and bury large sums of money which they had obtained while in the Caribbean.

Quelch was arrested and sentenced to death by hanging. On June 30, 1704, he was hung at the foot of Fleet Street in Boston, Massachusetts.

The Legend of Pirate Sandy Gordon's White Isle Treasure

Captain Sandy Gordon, a pirate who buried a huge treasure sometime between 1715 and 1718 on White Island has been best described as both mean and greedy. White Island is one of nine small outcroppings of rock which are the Isles of Shoals and are found about ten miles off the shores of both Maine and New Hampshire.

Gordon went to sea from his home in Scotland while still a boy. The first record of his nautical career was as a ship's carpenter aboard the *Porpoise,* an armed merchantman commanded by Captain John Herring. The captain was commissioned to capture Algerian corsairs who were creating havoc with British shipping in the area of the Barbary Coast.

Captain Has Daughter Aboard

It was against all nautical protocols of the day, but Captain Herring took his beautiful eighteen-year-old daughter Martha on this mission rather than leave her alone at home.

The *Porpoise* was not out of London but a few days when young Gordon began to make serious advances toward the golden-haired young maiden. Captain Herring soon caught wind of this and told Gordon to back off or face the venom of the cat-o-nine-tails.

Captain's Daughter

The young ship's carpenter heeded this warning for a few days, but Martha's beauty attracted him like a powerful magnet. In fact, it was not long thereafter that Herring trapped Gordon alone with the girl in the captain's cabin.

The father was furious. Seizing the young seaman by the throat, he threw him sprawling upon the deck and sentenced him to seventy-two lashes upon his bare back. In addition, he was clapped into irons and interred in the ships hold for thirty days to meditate over his perfidy.

When he finally returned to duty, Sandy went about his appointed tasks quietly and diligently, but this was only on the surface. Clandestinely, he was plotting a bold mutiny with certain unsavory members of the crew. As soon as a majority of the hands were ready to challenge Captain Herring, the conspiracy was ripe.

Mutiny on the Porpoise

Gordon selected a dark night when he was on watch. At a shot from Gordon's pistol, the mutineers seized control of the *Porpoise*, overwhelming Captain Herring and the loyal crewmen. The surprised master was hauled from his cabin and bound to a gun.

The punishment that Captain Herring had so recently meted out to Sandy was all too indelibly printed on the young sailor's mind. Seizing a lash, he evened the score then and there with seventy-two strokes upon the master's back. After several such beatings, spaced one hour apart, the Captain finally died and Gordon threw his body overboard.

Become a Pirate or be Thrown Overboard

At this point, Sandy locked Martha in the captain's cabin and forbade anyone to approach her. He gave everyone on board a choice, either turn pirate or be thrown overboard. The choice was easy to make. It was at this time that Gordon showed his greedy nature. His policy on this pirate ship was that there would be no division of plunder, as was the custom among buccaneers. All profits would be his. One slight concession was made, that the men would be paid wages twenty-five percent higher than those on merchant ships.

Fired as Captain, Expelled from the Ship

Now under the Jolly Roger, the ship sailed for some time off the coast of Scotland, capturing several valuable prizes. However, the crew grew exasperated

with Gordon's reaping all the profits while they risked life and limb. So it was not unexpected when they rebelled against Gordon. As a result, the pirates set Sandy and Martha adrift in a small boat and let them row for the Scottish coast. The two managed to find an old farm house as their home in the desolate coastal area.

Enter Blackbeard

It was at that time that the rascally Captain Edward Teach, called Blackbeard, Thatch, Tinch, or Drummond, and a small party visited this lonely shore in search of water, food, and liquor. When Teach came upon Gordon's humble abode, the latter did not have much to offer except lurid tales of his prowess as an adventurer and one-time pirate.

Come aboard my ship, said Teach, and I'll see how good a pirate you are. If you are as good as your boasting, I'll see you outfitted, and maybe we can do business together.

Soon after Gordon came aboard, the pirates sighted a richly laden East Indian ship, homeward bound for

London. Harold T. Wilkins in Pirate Treasure relates that the merchant ship put up a furious defense.

Gordon fought like a wild beast with cutlass and pistol until the merchantman's deck was clear of defenders. When the prize was finally secure, Teach slapped Gordon on the back and announced, Good work, lad. By your bravery today ye shown that ye deserve to be skipper of this prize. But mind you, all loot will be shared with the crew.

Made Captain by Blackbeard

Thus it was that Gordon renamed the ship the *Flying Scot*, and he and Teach set sail for the Spanish Main. This cruise was highly successful with both ships being well loaded with plunder. Eventually the two ships parted company, with an agreement to meet again at a future date among the Isles of Shoals.

Stopped to Pick up his Girlfriend

Following this agreement, Gordon sailed back to Scotland where he dropped anchor near his coastal farmhouse. He went ashore in a small boat and returned to his ship in the darkness of that night with the beautiful Martha in his arms. She was bound and carried kicking and screaming to the ship. Not a good way to begin the long journey to America.

On the cruise to America, the *Flying Scot* sighted a great Spanish galleon and gave chase. As the pirates drew near, the Spaniard let go with a broadside which was inaccurate enough to cause little damage. Meanwhile, the *Flying Scot* lived up to her name and pulled alongside the Spaniard. Grappling hooks were thrown to link the ships together, and then the buccaneers swarmed aboard their victim like a host of angry hornets.

Gordon played it safe and stood on his quarterdeck until his men had the situation well in hand. Now the time had come for him to leap aboard the merchantman and take the Spanish captain as his prisoner.

The galleons captain proved to be a very stubborn individual, but, after some highly persuasive measures, he revealed the amount of treasure on board and the secret places in which it was stored, and then he was thrown overboard. Gordon took more than a million dollars worth of gold and silver out of the Spanish vessel.

His Crew Buried their Loot on Star Island

The *Flying Scot* arrived at the Isles of Shoals several weeks before Captain Teach. Landing at Star Island, Gordon ordered a division of the treasure to be made. When this had been accomplished, *the crew broke up into several small groups to bury their shares of loot.*

What of Captain Gordon and the fair Martha? They took up residence a short distance away on White Island. Sandy had a small cottage built for them there, and it was near the cottage that he buried his treasure.

How much did he bury? This is anyone's guess, but most authorities agree that it was an amount of considerable value.

In time, Captain Teach arrived on the scene, and there was more burying of treasure. Teach is alleged to have cached as much as $300,000 on Star Island. Both he and Gordon held several conferences at this time, and when it was amicably agreed to dissolve their partnership, Teach took off for the Spanish Main.

Unfortunate Case of Mistaken Identity

A week or two later, a lookout spied a sail on the horizon. The lure for more booty was great, so Gordon hastily assembled the crew and lifted anchor. The

strange sail turned out to be a British man-o-war on a hunt for pirates. A long and fierce conflict followed in which the British ship finally silenced Gordon's guns. The vessels were locked together for the last stage of the conflict, when a tremendous explosion rent the air, strewing the sea with the fragments of both ships.

Stung to madness by defeat and knowing that, if taken alive, he would be gallows bait, Sandy Gordon fired the *Flying Scots* magazine, sending himself and his merry men to eternity. His girlfriend and his treasure remained somewhere on White Island.

Spanish Galleon Runs Aground on Star Island

Some early records from Spain indicate that a Spanish galleon had crashed on the eastern shore of Star Island around 1685, at a spot known as Miss Underhill's Chair. This galleon

Spanish Galleon

carried a substantial amount of gold coins, silver place, and silver bullion. Incidentally, the Cosport Church, located on Star Island, was constructed partly of timbers from this galleon.

On the western side of the island there was once an old fort that was protected by nine cannons. Although the cannons have since been removed, the area of the fort itself is a good metal detecting site for relics, coins, and the like.

Appledore Silver Ship Disaster

In the 18th century, Appledore Island was the scene of a terrible silver ship disaster in which sailors managed to get ashore with a substantial amount of the bullion that had been aboard. The history of the sailors has been lost in the years, but there have been many cases of people finding silver coins on or near the ledges along the eastern side of the island.

Wentworth by the Sea Treasure

New Castle - Since the Portsmouth Journal article of 1882 was published there have been rumors of treasure buried somewhere between the Little Harbor Bridge, near the Wentworth Hotel, and the island upon which is found a cottage owned by a Charles E. Campbell.

According to the article: *"a party of Boston men had a diver at work at New Castle, searching for alleged treasures in the bed of the river lying nearly midway between the bridge leading to the Wentworth, and the island on which the Charles E. Campbell cottage was located."*

In its first account, the Journal said the searchers dragging the mud of Little Harbor were guided *"by revelations made in a document in their possession, over one hundred years old, and whose authenticity is undoubted, the full contents of*

Dowsing for Treasure

which the holders decline to disclose. The work of diving for the expected 'fortune' has been in quiet progress, off and on for several months, and is to be continued indefinitely, but the results thus far of the investigations at the bottom, are kept a profound secret."

The following week the Journal reported: *"The information about the alleged treasure had came from an elderly New Castle resident. Before his death two years earlier, the man had alluded to a treasure map hidden in the lining of one of his vests. It would lead to three chests of gold, a barrel filled with silver and a box of coins."*

On May 5, 1883, a professional dowser from Belfast, Maine was hired to find the treasure "whose divining rod played fantastic tricks over the same spot that other diviners had found."

Has the treasure been found or is it perhaps buried along Campbell's Lane waiting to be found?

Clergyman's Gold and a Goat

New Castle – The New York Mail, provides yet another story of treasure in New Castle: *"There has been more or less gossip for a long time in reference to a fabulous amount of money said to be buried in New Castle, Little Harbor. The story of the hidden treasure has, perhaps, for its foundation some facts; at least there are those who accept the visionary tale about buried treasure on our shore, and at different times within the past three years a systematic search for the still unfound gold has been instituted.*

Those most directly interested in the affair are very reticent when interrogated relative to the story. It is affirmed that many years ago a wealthy clergyman set sail from England, bringing along a large sum of money, which he proposed, as became his benevolent nature, to use in benefiting our fore-fathers in the name of his Creator."

Clergyman's island companion

"Those on board the vessel in which he embarked learned of the wealth on board, and resolved to have control of it. To attain this end the clergyman was forcibly put off the vessel and placed upon one of the

Isles of Shoals, and bearing with him for companionship a goat. The crew sailed away, but on account of a severe storm was obliged to put into Little Harbor. How, why or when the gold was buried, or by whom, are points not made clear in the narrative as told to your correspondent. A chart showing the locality of the yet unearthed gold fell into the hands of a school teacher, who, while on a journey, was taken sick, and sought the hospitality of a family in a Maine town. His sickness proved a fatal one, and just before dying he informed his kind friends that he could only repay their kindness by presenting them with a chart which would indicate where much wealth was concealed, and stated that the chart was sewed up in the lining of his vest."

Man's vest

New York article pinpoints the treasure site:

"The party who is now engaged in the search is A.J. Griffin, of Melrose. By marrying into the family, he came into possession of the chart in question, which located the money at one and a half miles below Portsmouth, on the west side of Newcastle Island, 25 rods below the bridge, 20 rods below Black Point at low water, where there is a rock 3 x 4 feet, with the formation of a windowsill on top; on the east side is a barrel of silver and on the west three chests of gold. There are two objects which the chart specifies that cannot be found, namely; the 3 x 4 foot rock and the bridge spoken of."

Is the Gold Still There to be Found?

Fur Trader's Treasure

The coins are supposed to have belonged to A less than honest fur trader by the name of John Cromwell established an outpost in Merrimack about 1665. His trading post was located on the rocky shore near Cromwell's Falls on the Merrimack River.

Fur trader

Cromwell was constantly cheating the Indians and they finally had enough and planned to attack and burn his trading post in retaliation for his crookedness. Somehow Cromwell "got wind" of their plans and hurriedly buried his money of gold and silver coins and took off planning to return after things cooled down and retrieve his bounty.

Cromwell never did return and his ill-gotten treasure lies in the ground somewhere near Cromwell Falls on the Merrimack River.

Finding Treasure in

Massachusetts

Where it has been found and

Where you can find more

Pirate Treasure Chests at Balance Rock

Pittsfield - This legend is about pirate treasure. Yes, pirate treasure far from the sea in the Berkshires of western Massachusetts.

The legend has an attorney and an accomplice stealing two chests filled with gold and silver coins from a pirate. Additional details regarding the theft are scant. The value was estimated to be $200,000 at the time; more than 3 Million today.

They are reported to have buried the two boxes near a large, unique rock upon which they carved a letter "A"

Balance Rock in Balance Rock State Park

for identification upon their return, which they never did. One can only imagine why they left their nefariously obtained fortune unclaimed.

One chest has reportedly been found near Balance Rock in the 1930's; the second still undiscovered.

Driving directions to park gate: From Rt 7 in Lanesboro, go left on Bull Hill Rd., which turns into Naragansett Ave. Then take a right on Balance Rock Rd. Gate is about a mile up the road.

Dungeon Rock Cave

Lynn –This place has it all; pirates, treasure and ghosts. It's the story of a cave dug by a man directed by ghosts to find pirate treasure

Stairs leading down into the cave

Legend tells of pirate Thomas Veale burying several chests containing gold and silver coins nearby or inside the cave. Veale was living in the cave when an earthquake hit the area and he was killed. The knowledge of exactly where his treasure chests were hidden died with him.

In 1852, Hiram Marble, a spiritualist, bought the cave and built a house and outbuildings on the spot. He moved his wife and son to the area and began excavating a new cave to retrieve the treasure. Marble believed he was receiving directions to the treasure from the ghost of Thomas Veale himself

Hiram passed away in 1868 without ever finding his treasure. His son Edwin dug on until his death in 1880. Edwin's last wish was to be buried at Dungeon Rock. At the top of a set of stairs beginning next to the old cellar hole, you will find a large pink piece of rock. This stone marks the grave of Edwin Marble and the end of the quest for treasure..

1,000 Buildings Burn to the Ground

Chelsea - On a sunny and windy Palm Sunday morning in 1908, a smoker casually dumped his pipe's hot ashes near an open lot used to dry rags at the corner of Second and Carter streets.

Chelsea was a wealthy town at the time and the great fire burned half of the town to the ground.

The fire left 19 dead and the survivors homeless and all of their possessions gone; including the gold and silver coins and precious jewelry.

This area is a potential treasure trove of hidden artifacts and treasure that were presumed destroyed.

In 1921 a workman discovered a box containing $50,000, $725,000 today, in Gold, silver coins and silverware in the area where the "Great Fire" burned all.

Treasure of Grey Court Castle

Methuen - Greycourt State Park is the former site of Charles H. Tenney's Grey Court Castle. The estate's gatehouse is now home to the Methuen Historical Society.

Grey Court (aka Tenney Castle)

The legend of the castle includes the infamous Tenney brother's feud over a woman, drug rehabilitation, a suicidal monk and a haunted gatehouse.

A treasure cache is rumored to be hidden somewhere on the estate. In 1930 $20,000, with an estimated value today of $450,000, in negotiable bonds was discovered on the property. This is an ideal situation to employ your dowsing skill; metal detectors will not find paper money or bonds but your dowsers sure can.

The Corrill Brothers Fortune

Methuen -. Nathaniel and Mark Corrill's home is located on "Daddy Frye's" Hill; not far from Tenney Castle.

This legend involves another brotherly feud over a young lady. Could it be the same woman over which their neighbors, the Tenney brothers, became estranged? In any event, the fact remains that the brothers both fell in love with the same woman.

However, she was not interested in either of the brothers and in fact married another while the brothers fought.

The marriage did not end their feud and they never again spoke to one another for the rest of their lives even though they were living in the same house. It is said that they individually became quite wealthy amassing sizeable fortunes.

When the brothers died, it was reported that they had hidden several caches of gold coins. None of these has been found, as far as can be determined. It is believed that part of their treasure was hidden around

Buried in a backyard

Tenney Castle, as well as on their homestead. It is very likely that at least two, if not more, caches were made as the brothers refused to speak to each other, and they are sure to have buried their respective fortunes in different sites.

Plum Island

Plum Island - In 1943 a German submarine surfaced one moonless night and sent a rubber raft, full of Nazis, ashore. Their mission was to perform acts of sabotage on sensitive US assets. They brought with them a box containing $200,000 in US currency; money that would be used to fund their nefarious plans.

Plum Island sand dunes

Somehow the raft capsized in Atlantic surf all, but one, of the Nazi saboteurs drowned and never made it to shore. The lone survivor buried the box of money in the sandy dunes.

He made his way of the beach, and because he spoke perfect English, was able to blend in with the American population. He eventually made his way to Wisconsin, later becoming a U.S. citizen.

He returned to Plum Island in 1960 hoping to retrieve the treasure box. He remembered only that he had secreted the cache on the Atlantic side of the Island. Search as he did, the money was never found.

Is this a job for a dowser to complete?

Short Beach and Grover's Cliff

Winthrop – Grover's Cliff is the "Highland section of Winthrop near the entrance to Boston Harbor and the location of Fort Heath. Although the fort's military structures have been replaced by a residential complex, Small Park remains open land and a likely spot to find ancient relics.

Grover's Cliff in Winthrop

The really exciting spot to search however is the beach below the bluff. It is here that many Spanish and British coins dating from the eighteenth century have been found in the sand. The area between Short Beach and Grover's Cliff seems to be the most prolific.

It is theorized that the coins have come from the many ships that have been wrecked off the north side of Boston Harbor. Treasure has been appearing along this stretch for centuries, especially after severe nor'easters.

How much treasure is left and how much longer will it continue to be washed ashore no one knows.

Captain Horton's Silver

Winthrop - On the morning of November 28, 1682, a ship whose name is forgotten was shattered on what is now known as Winthrop Bar in Boston Harbor near Winthrop's "Five Sisters". The ship, commanded by a Captain Horton, was carrying a valuable cargo of silver bullion en route from the West Indies to Boston.

Captain Horton sailed into Massachusetts Bay during a severe blizzard that made it nearly impossible to navigate. Losing direction, the ship was known to have skirted past the Brewster Islands late in the night of November 27. On the morning of November 28, near the present city of Winthrop, Captain Horton lost his ship on the bar.

Sunken silver bars

Three of the 13 sailors were washed over the side and drowned. Ten of the men reached shore and began walking along Shirley Gut Plain. Half frozen, they began dropping one by one, and only six managed to reach the house of Dean Winter. There they found food, warmth, and shelter, and managed to survive.

Captain Horton was lost with his silver cargo and the mystery of the sunken silver ship has never been solved. The wreck is somewhere along Winthrop Bar. Attempts at finding it have failed, and the ship and her silver fortune still await salvage.

Revolutionary Hessian Loot

Dalton – During the Revolutionary War Hessian (German) mercenaries found themselves in peril of being captured by the Colonialists. They therefore collected all of their valuables and placed them into a howitzer which the secretively buried in the woods.

The plan was, they would return and retrieve the valuables after the war or when it was safe to do so. They never did return and their treasure-laden howitzer is buried in the woods alongside a Dalton road.

Hessian mercenaries in a New England town

There are only two significant roads in Dalton along which they would have been travelling, route 8 and route 8A. Perhaps a search first using your dowsing abilities to pinpoint, the hopefully still woods, where they buried their valuables.

Gallops Island

Boston Harbor – This 23 acre island lies 10 miles out of Boston and is named after John Gallop, one of Boston Harbor's first pilots, who lived on the island.

Gallop's Island

Since then the island has been occupied by a restaurant and inn and a quarantine station. During the Civil War a military camp housing 3,000 Union soldiers occupied the island, and during World War II a radio school and also a school for bakers and cooks was on the Island. All of this activity on such a compact space makes the island prime treasure hunting territory.

Most intriguing of all is the legend that the famous Captain Kidd, before his capture in 1699, may have buried treasure here. In addition to Captain Kidd's pirate treasure the pirate Henry Avery supposedly hid a cache of diamonds on the island.

Dubbed "The Arch Pirate" and "The King of Pirates," Avery was the most notorious pirate of his time; he earned his infamy by becoming one of the few major pirate captains to retire without being arrested or killed in battle

Metal detectors will not find diamonds however those with dowsing skill very well might. Good luck.

137

Choate Island

Essex - Choate Island, also known as Hog Island, is located in the Essex River Estuary in Essex, Massachusetts. It is part of the Crane Wildlife Refuge, which is owned and managed by The Trustees of Reservations.

A wealthy retired English businessman named John Wilson Breed converted his money into several chests gold and silver coins and sailed for America.   He purchased the island, then named Hog Island, and built his retirement home there.

The homestead on Choate Island

The island had many caves in which he could secret his treasure. All that is known of the whereabouts of his cave is that he is said to have told his wife "I have found the perfect hiding location." It was a cave "located less than a quarter mile from the house" but one that offered protection and concealment for his gold and silver. Despite her protestations, he never disclosed the location of the cave to her.

In 1846 Breed suffered a massive and unexpected heart attack and died instantly; the location of his treasure dying with him.

Pirate Treasure at Blue Rock

Chappaquiddick Island – On a summer evening in 1824 James Roland Cooke, an aged, recluse farmer, was walking in the dunes near Cape Poge when he came upon a strange happening.

He peered over the crest of dune to see five men; they appeared to be pirates, who had come ashore in a skiff, burying what looked like a treasure chest. When the digging was finished and the chest lowered the three men in the hole where shot by their companions.

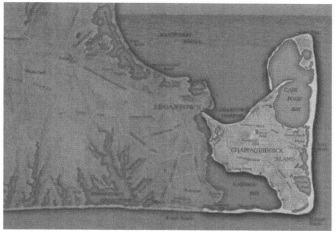

Chappaquiddick Island

The dead pirates were buried along with the treasure and the two murderous scoundrels rowed off around the bluff toward the mainland.

Cooke scurried back to his abode afraid the pirates might return. The next morning he went back to the spot identified by the large blue rock that was near where the treasure chest was buried.

Search and dig as he would, day after day, he could not find the treasure box. Too bad he didn't have any dowsing equipment at his disposal; but you do.

139

Inland Pirate Treasure

Maynard – During a spring storm in 1720 a group of men came to the residence of Thomas Smith requesting shelter from a storm. Smith offered them his barn in which they stayed for several days.

Before they left they bought some old clothing from the Smiths and made sacks out of them. They also asked to borrow a few shovels.

Gold and silver coins

As they left it was apparent that the sacks were loaded with something heavy as they were headed in the direction of the Assabet River. Some time later the men returned without the sacks, thanked the Smiths, left and were never seen again.

A few months later Smith received a letter from a man who stated that he was part of the group that Smith had let stay in his barn that spring. He confessed that they all were pirates and that they had been captured and convicted of piracy. They all were now awaiting hanging and requested Smith come to Boston to see them, promising to give him some information that would be of value. Smith ignored the request and the pirates were hung taking the knowledge of their treasure's location to their graves.

The location of the old Smith house is unknown but is thought to have been somewhere along the Assabet River in what is now Maynard's Riverside Park. Perhaps the gold and silver coins are buried there.

Ghost Town Treasure

Cape Anne – The ghost town, once known as "Common Settlement" and now "Dogtown", is divided between Gloucester and Rockport. It was settled, beginning in 1693, partly because its inland location afforded protection from pirates and from enemy natives.

Treasure of all kinds can be found here, including rare Colonial coins, china, pottery, brass belt buckles, gold rings, nails, knives, sundials, pewter spoons and forks, sewing thimbles, bottles, and arrowheads.

The peak of population, from 1750-1800, is estimated at around 100 families. At the conclusion of the War of 1812, because of the lingering fear of coastal bombardment, and poor soil conditions, most

Colonial coins, rings, shot etc.

farmers moved away from Dogtown. For a few decades itinerants and vagabonds, occupied their abandoned houses giving the area a bad reputation.

Many of the widows of sea-goers and soldiers who never returned kept dogs for protection and company. As these last inhabitants died their pets became feral, roaming the moors and howling, possibly giving rise to the nickname "Dogtown."

The land is held in trust by Gloucester and Rockport and is therefore protected in perpetuity. Dogtown affords rich recreation opportunities to hikers and bikers, dog-walkers, nature lovers, cross-country skiers, geologists, treasure hunters and historians.

Much of Dogtown is now dense woodland, crisscrossed and bisected by trails and old roads. Dogtown Road off of Cherry Street in the western section (the Gloucester side) is lined with the remains of the cellar holes of the settlers, many of which are numbered in correspondence with names from John J. Babson's book of the history of Gloucester.

Babson's grandson, Roger Babson, is known for, among other things, his commissioning of unemployed

One of Babson's 38 stones

stonecutters to carve inspirational inscriptions on thirty eight boulders in Dogtown during the Great Depression. Babson also mapped and numbered the cellar holes left from the homes of Dogtown's former residents.

The northwest corner of Dogtown is the Norton Memorial forest and covers 121 acres. This land is named for Frederick Norton, a NASA physicist and MIT professor whose family owned land on the outskirts of Dogtown. Beginning in the 1930s, Norton planted more than a 100,000 trees and forty different species of ferns there, and also forged and maintained trails nearby.

Grey's Raid 1778

Martha's Vineyard - September 10, 1778, British General Charles Grey in command of a transport of eighty-two ships and ten thousand British troops made a raid upon the Vineyard at Vineyard Haven.

Grey's forces confiscated 10,000 sheep, 300 oxen, many cows and swine plus the local militia's arms as well as most of the island's weapons and £950 of "Public Funds."

Grey's fleet approaches Martha's Vineyard

Grey landed small contingents of troops on September 12 to accelerate the process and to destroy vessels found in the area. Four islanders were killed and sixteen missing in the encounter.

Islanders were in fear of both life and property. Island legend relates the story of an elderly woman who, living alone, hastened to gather up her valuables and money at first sight of the British men-o-war. She buried her valuables near her home.

The woman survived Gray's raid, and indeed, survived the entire Revolutionary War. Perhaps her age, or the turmoil of the situation at hand, explains her inability to remember just where she buried her money and valuables. She searched for them diligently, even enlisting the aid of her neighbors. But to her dismay, she had hidden the cache so well that she could never find it.

That the woman lived near Beck's Pond is written fact, although history does not supply us with her name. A map of the island today shows numerous ponds, but none of them is known as Beck's Pond. Back in the day, when property changed hands the pond usually became known by the new owner's name.

Map dowsing to identify which of the Vineyard's many ponds was once named Beck's Pond would be a good starting point in uncovering this ancient treasure.

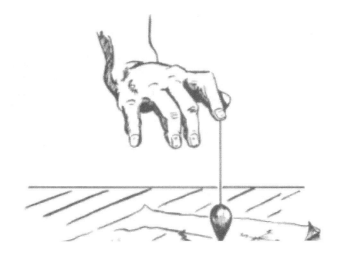

Gold Bullion and Gold

Nantucket - According to an ancient American Indian legend, sometime before the white man settled on Nantucket a French sailing ship was blown ashore near Sesachacha Pond on the Siasconset side of the island.

French gold bullion and coins

On board was a large quantity of gold bullion and coinage. The sailors were able to salvage the treasure, which they are believed to have buried near where they came ashore.

This story has been related for generations and many have scoured the beaches in search of the treasure; but is it on the sandy beach? Probably not.

Most of the land around Sesachacha Pond is still undeveloped. Could the French gold still be there awaiting discovery?

Pirate Treasure?

Westport - James M. Eddy, was searching for the pirate Captain Kidd's treasure and found a treasure buried by someone else instead. Just who it was that buried the treasure is still unknown.

According to local legend Eddy owned a farm adjoining Horseneck Beach in Westport, Massachusetts. Eddy began his search in 1886 using an old parchment map thought to have belonged to his grandfather who,

many old-timers believed, was once a pirate himself.

The map was made from a drumhead and the lines on the map, drawn with a sharp, pointed object.

Pot of silver coins

The map showed the locations of three separate caches of gold, silver, jewelry and other treasures where the pirates had buried their treasure more than one hundred years earlier.

Eddy began his secretive search at a large rock on Horseneck Point as indicated on his map. He had been searching for more than a year when he uncovered a pot full of Spanish silver coins.

The coins were dated from 1781 to 1851, and therefore not part of Captain Kidd's much-sought treasure as Kidd was hanged in London on May 24, 1701.

According to the map two more caches remain. One contains gold coins, while another diamonds and jewels. There is no record of Eddy locating the two other pots so perhaps they are waiting for you to find them.

Roaring Bulls Gold

Boston's Outer Harbor - The Roaring Bulls are two rock outcrops between Green Island and the Graves. These rocks are especially deadly because they lie just under the waterline at high tide. The water's depth ranges fro 10 to 50 feet and is usually clear.

In 1851on a cold winter night, the French ship Fleur d'Or, a twin-masted brigantine, left the port of St Malo headed for America.

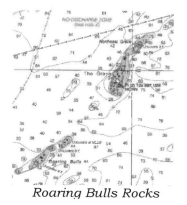
Roaring Bulls Rocks

She was loaded with textiles and casks of wine, but her crew made no move to put out to sea. In his cabin, the captain impatiently awaited the arrival of a special cargo; two iron chest containing 15 bricks each of solid gold. It took twelve muscular men to load the chests onto the ship.

The value of the gold at that time was $420,00, which translates into many millions today.

As the Fleur d'Or approached Boston, the weather deteriorated. Soon, the ship was completely enveloped in a blinding blizzard.

Suddenly, the treasure-laden brigantine ran up on the submerged Roaring Bulls Rocks in Boston Bay. The captain and his crew were thrown into the icy waters and miraculously all were able to make it to Graves Island. They were rescued a few days later hungry, frost bitten but alive.

The ship was torn to pieces and the 30 bars of gold fell onto the rocky bottom. Scuba diving was not developed for another 100 years and therefore no salvage attempts were made.   Is there gold on Roaring Bulls or is this just a fable?

147

King of Calf Island's Treasure

Strong Island is located in Pleasant Bay on Cape Cod and is owned by the Chatham Conservation Foundation.

The King of Calf Island was a keeper of Bug Light in Boston Harbor. He retired to live a solitary life on Calf Island, further out to sea in Boston Harbor until his death in 1882.

The King of Calf Island

It was rumored that he was once a pirates who had ravaged the West Indies early in the 19th Century, had come to the U.S. from Canada after murdering a man with a barrel stave.

He also reportedly has hid $500,000 in gold coin on Strong Island, $1,900 of which has been found by Edward Rowe Snow, writer, historian and adventurer.

Here is one version of Snow's adventure:
"Somehow Snow got the idea that the King must have left a chart showing the exact location of his treasure, which was supposed to be worth about $500,000. He didn't find the chart, but he did get hold of an old book in Italian which local tradition said had belonged to the King. Snow took the book to the Boston Public Library for appraisal.

"Now comes the part of the story that reads like fiction, but the facts were reported by the Boston papers and retold in Time Magazine, on October 15, 1945. According to Time's account, the old Italian book was turned over to Harriet Swift of the Boston Public Library. She turned the leaves and noticed a pattern of pin-holes on page 101. The holes pierced letters, forming a simple coded message. Its exciting message: The King of Calf Island had buried a treasure on Strong Island, off the shore of Cape Cod.

"When this coded message was explained to him, Edward Snow and his brother Donald set out for Strong Island at once. The pin pricks evidently did not tell exactly where the stuff was buried, but Snow took along an electronic gadget similar to a mine detector, which is used in locating metals. The Snow brothers dug five holes in the sand, and each time they found metal; but it proved to be only iron from some old wreck. But in the sixth excavation they hit the jackpot, according to Time, when the mean unearthed a small, encrusted copper box. It was full of tarnished old coins, minted in Peru,

Snow with his Strong Island coins

Mexico, Portugal, France, and Spain. Time carried a picture of Edward Snow sitting in the sand, with the box open in front of him, and both hands full of coins. The treasure amounted to only about $1,900.

While this was quite a treasure in 1945, the big question to a modern-day treasure hunter is, where is the remaining supposed $498,000 that the King of Calf Island is believed to have hidden? As far as can be learned, nothing else has been found."

Mill River Dam Break

Williamsburg/Northampton-

In May 16,1874 the Mill River reservoir dam burst, sending an avalanche of water down a narrow valley lined with homes, factories and farms. Within an hour, 139 people were dead, and four mill villages were washed away leaving 740 homeless.

None of the villages in the Mill River valley between Williamsburg and Northampton that were washed away ever returned to their former greatness, and today much of the land is mostly wooded.

Aftermath of the flood

The valley is littered with silver coins, personal jewelry, household instruments, tools, and other paraphernalia, much of which are within a few inches of the surface of the ground

A chest containing $7,000 (1874 dollars) in gold and silver coin is known to have been washed away somewhere between Haydenville and Florence. It probably is not the only family strong box to have been washed away and buried in the silt. The safe from a Haydeville bank was also washed away and is yet to be recovered.

Treasure of the "Holy Ghost"

Nantasket, Hull

In 1653 a Dutch privateer (legal pirate) from Amsterdam with the curious name of *De Heylige Gheest* (Holy Ghost), was harassing Spanish shipping along the coast of Central America. The privateers amassed a large fortune in gold, pearls, precious stones, and Spanish pieces-of-eight.

While resupplying in the Barbados the privateers were attacked by pirates who killed them all and set sail for parts unknown. Much later the pirates were spotted in distress off Cape Cod, by a passing ship, the *Juno*. They were without food or water, many were sick. The *Juno* provided them with the needed food and water and escorted them towards Boston.

Spanish treasure

They dropped anchor off Nantasket for a few days before authorities, suspecting they were pirates or in any event undesirables, demanded they leave Boston Harbor. Arriving in Salem the pirates were captured as a ship from the Barbados alerted officials of their piratical actions there. The sailors were imprisoned, the *Holy Ghost* impounded and searched; no treasure was found.

During the trial testimony confirmed the facts that the ship contained a treasure trove *"consisting of a chest six feet long, filled with gold, another chest of jewels and pearls, and seven hogsheads of pieces-of-eight, beside all other traffic."*

The treasure has yet to be found.

151

Belcher's Cave

Great Barrington

Quoted from "NEW ENGLAND'S BURIED TREASURE"
by Clay Perry, 1946

Literally and figuratively the cave was the first underworld hideout of the criminal. In the year 1765 a man who went by the name of Gill Belcher migrated from Hebron, Connecticut, to the town of Great Barrington, Massachusetts, and there set up as a silversmith. It is possible that he traveled up through Connecticut by way of Enfield, for later there was associated with him, in an enterprise which caused no small stir about southern New England and eastern New York State, a young man called William Hulburt or Hubbard, son of an estimable Enfield man, Obadiah Hubbard.

At any rate, Gill Belcher, a family man, who eight years later stated that he had "nine small children, the eldest twelve, and an aged mother" of whom he was an only son, made his appearance in June in the pretty little Housatonic River town in the Berkshire Hills and soon bought an interesting piece of property. It was a bit of a rocky hill, rising about 250 feet above the highway, later know as Knox Trail, where it joins the present U.S. Highway No. 7 at the northwestern edge of the town.

This property had been owned by an eccentric gentleman, a veteran of the French Wars and prominent in military and civic affairs, William King, Jr., a major in the Revolutionary War. By its humorous owner, the property was called "Bung Hill" at the time he sold it to Belcher. On the side of the solid stone eminence was a cave, "halfway up a steep, jagged declivity on the north face of Bung Hill" which was a bold, unevenly rounded knob of rocks covered in part with a scanty growth of trees and with massive blocks of stone strewn along its base.

152

There seemed nothing strange about this purchase of land, because at the northern base of the hill, on a little level of land, was a small house where Belcher settled himself and family and proceeded to engage in his trade as a workman in silver and gold. Doubtless Mr. King considered himself well rid of the rocky hill which was sometimes haunted by rattlesnakes, sunning themselves and by various wild animals.

Counterfeit coins

The cave itself is an immense opening in the hillside, evidently formed by some ancient convulsion of nature, one of those geological "faults" which form grottoes in the hard rock, in some localities. The portal yawns high and wide but the passage soon narrows and a heap of fallen rocks in fragments forms a barrier rising waist high, beyond which is a chamber about thirty feet long and eight to ten feet wide. This is roofed by one solid sheet or block of stone more than fifty feet long which forms also the eastern wall, like an attic room with the peak of the roof ten to fifteen feet about the floor, but at the side, bearing down to nothing.

Across the top of the outer entrance is a spearlike blade of stone which, in some lights and at some angles, resembles a huge scimitar or sabre; and in others a rude replica of an elephant's trunk.

153

The inner room is dimly lighted through an opening about midway of its length near the top and also by a smaller aperature - this latter seeming to have served a great many times as a chimney, for the blackened walls about it testify to fire.

That there had been many a fire there in the time of Gill Belcher, and for a nefarious purpose, was established several years after he had taken up his abode at Bung Hill. He sold the property in 1768 but is believed to have carried on his trade of silver-smithing at the house for some time afterward. At any rate, when he was committed to jail for counterfeiting on October

The cave

30, 1772, it is a matter of record that he was taken while he and others were in the cave, engaged in manufacturing counterfeits in imitation of "York money"; that is, coins and currency bearing the official imprint and accepted as standard in the Province of New York - and in the provinces of New England also.

On October 30, 1772, militiamen surrounded the cave with muskets, pointing toward the entrance and demanding that Belcher and his partner, "Ugly" Lovely, come out and surrender.

The two confederates quickly stashed all the silver and damning evidence which they could into a pre-arranged hiding place. The men were arrested and taken to Albany, where they were later hanged. It is entirely credible to suppose that silver for use in the counterfeiting operation may still be hidden somewhere nearby, for none has ever been reported found.

Greylock Mountain Treasures

North Adams - In 1765 a group of counterfeiters known as the "Money Brook " gang operated out of a cave located on the North Adams side of Greylock Mountain somewhere along Money Brook.

1753 Spanish coins

They were making counterfeit Spanish dollars and Pine Tree shillings when a local hunter discovered them. He slipped away and reported the illegal activity to authorities.

The counterfeiters were captured but no coins were found. They had successfully hidden the coins somewhere. They were tried, found guilty and hung without revealing where their cache was hidden.

The Quaker Gold Mine Shaft

A man known as Uncle Billy Badger, a pioneer mineralogist, was supposed to have found a gold vein somewhere in the mountain.

He died unexpectedly and took the knowledge of the gold mine's location to his grave. The Quaker Gold Mine Shaft is supposed to be in the Notch area of the mountains.

Buried Box of Coins

West Chesterfield – In W. C. Jameson's book "Buried Treasures of New England" the tale of a farmer back in the 17th century and his buried stash of coins.

Indians frequently attacked Alden Culver. He survived many attacks and to protect his money he buried it in a locked box in the woods near his farmstead.

One legend says he added personal items of value to him, in addition to his money, and asked a friend to place the box of coins in his casket along with him when he died.

When he passed, the friend buried him with his lock box. Later, his daughter passed away and the friend buried her next to him. He had inscribed their names on a rock nearby.

Box of coins

Another version has the daughter substituting the valuables in her father's treasure box for stones and that it is this box that was buried with her father.

She allegedly reburied the coins and other valuables near the well, or some other place, at the back of the family's farmhouse. She died suddenly without telling anyone where she hid the box and was buried next to her father in the family plot.

It is unlikely that this tale will result in your finding buried boxes of coins in West Chesterfield. It does however, illustrate the usual practice of hiding valuables in the ground, wells, foundations etc.

Went Down With a Cargo of Gold Bullion

Cape Cod - In the last week of January 1942, the
Adair sailed with a cargo of spare aircraft parts, other
military supplies, and $30,000 in gold bullion ($32 an
ounce at the time), meant to finance American troops
purchase of goods in Iceland. She sailed east to clear
Long Island, and then headed north for Newfoundland.
Her captain and crew were unaware that a German
submarine, the U-123, was waiting off Cape Cod.

Adair goes down

Hardegen, captain of the U-123, brought his
submarine to the surface; the *Adair* was clearly
silhouetted against the lights dogging the coastline,
and the Germans spotted her.

He fired a single torpedo that exploded directly
beneath the *Adair's* hull, snapping her cleanly in half.
Flames from the exploding ship lit the sky for miles,
and the *U-123* quickly submerged and retreated
southward. Within minutes the *Adair* sank, with all
hands, in deep water off Cape Cod, taking the bullion
and her officers and crew down with her.

It has remained unsalvaged to this day.

The Old Fort Treasure

Located somewhere in the town of Shirley, is an estimated $400,000 in gold and silver coins.

The Fort Shirley Treasure

Construction of the fort began in July of 1744 at the direction of Governor Shirley. It was completed in October 1744. The fort was 60 feet square with 11 foot wide barracks and mounts that were 12 foot square and 7 feet high.

Old Willard Tavern

This fort was one of a line of forts along the northwest corner of Massachusetts built during King George's War and it was the first headquarters for this line of forts.

The colonial militia built it, and it saw no action, and was therefore ordered dismantled in 1754 as it was badly located for defense. The fort is located near Hosmer Road in Shirley is marked with granite monument erected in1901. It was excavated in 1974.

There is a legend alleging that a hoard of gold and silver coins are buried near the site of the old Willard Tavern in Shirley, now the Bull Run Tavern, where Parker Road meets Route 2A. The hoard is claimed to be in valued at $400,000 in 18th century dollars.

Chatham Beach Gold

In 1831 Chatham Beach fisherman Arthur Doane received permission to go ashore for a short visit with his fiance with the understanding that he would be rejoining his ship at four o'clock in the morning at North Chatham Beach. Sometime after midnight, Doane was making his way along the shoreline when he came upon a group of men who were obviously pirates burying a large iron chest.

Doane hid himself among the dunes until dawn when he emerged and used a piece of driftwood to unearth the chest. It turned out to be filled with numerous sacks of gold Spanish coins.

Chatham Beach

The fisherman was now a millionaire, and he immediately began to think like one. Lucky Arthur Doane removed the sacks of gold, then dragged the chest to a new location, and reburied it and replaced most of the loot.

Later Doane worked out an arrangement with his friend John Eldridge to sell a few coins out of state each month, thereby avoiding undue attention. The arrangement lasted 49 years until Doane became too ill to retrieve the coins himself and had to confide the secret location of the cache to Eldridge. When Eldridge was finally given directions to the treasure location, greed got the better of him, and he removed and sold an entire sack of coins, leaving only six sacks of gold in the dwindling cache.

A very angry and upset Arthur Doane died a short time later. However, when Eldridge returned to Chatham Beach to reclaim the remaining six sacks for himself, he found that a severe storm had completely re-arranged the beach, and he was unable to relocate the chest. He searched for several years but never found the treasure.

Spanish gold coins found on the beach

From time to time golden coins of Spanish origin have been found along the beach near old Chatham Lighthouse after storms. No one knows if the source of these finds is some off shore shipwreck or Arthur Doane's storm-tossed cache.

Trailside Museum, Blue Hills

There was gold found in the early 1900's in the Blue Hills. It is on display at the Trailside Museum, Canton.

Money Bluff on Deer Island

People have been searching for treasure on Deer Island since 1824, when a Captain Tewksbury, Rev. Brown, and Captain Crooker began digging (unsuccessfully) at Money Bluff in hopes of locating a lost hoard of gold. The island was said to be a storage location used by plundering pirates

Money Bluff

The
Whydah
The Story Behind the Largest Pirate Treasure Ever Found

(and it's off a Cape Cod beach)

Shipwrecks, Witches, Treachery, Sunken Treasure and, Ghosts

"Black" Sam Bellamy

Painting by Don Maitz

Samuel Bellamy was born in Devonshire, England in 1689. In the early 1700s, as a young teen, he left England to seek his fortune in the West Indies where he joined Captain Jennings and the British privateer fleet then at war against Spain. He was berthed aboard the sloop *Barsheba* and based at Port Royal in Jamaica.

Privateers were pirates by another name and were sponsored by their government. They were provided "Letters of Marque" which gave them the authorization to "pirate" ships free from fear of punishment in the event of their capture.

Sam Bellamy was a large black-haired man. He is reported to have been an intelligent and popular leader of men with a reputation for being generous to his victims. Some would later refer to him as the "Prince of Pirates".

It was probably during time spent in the Caribbean that he heard the stories of fantastic wealth lying on the bottom of the sea just waiting to be found. Tales of sunken Spanish treasure that would make a man richer than any king in Europe were standard seaman issue of the era.

It was here that he also was exposed to strategies and techniques he would later use during his short and very successful pirating career in the Caribbean.

He left his wife and child in Cantebury, England.. He would go back to the Caribbean, retrieve the legendary Spanish treasures and return a rich man.

His original plan was to locate and retrieve treasurer from a fleet of Spanish galleons that were known to have sunk off the Florida coast. For nearly one hundred years tales of a sunken Spanish galleon fleet laden with silver and gold had flamed the imagination of adventuresome young men in Europe. Perhaps the most famous of these stories was of Philip IV's treasure ship fleet heavily laden with riches that was destroyed in a great storm as it began its return to Spain.

Spanish Treasure Ship

King Philip IV depended upon the gold, silver, and copper treasures extracted from Spain's mines in the New World to fund his vast military establishment. However, the fleet of 1622 was delayed in sailing and left Havana at the height of the hurricane season. The entire fleet was lost when it sailed into the teeth of a violent hurricane. Remnants of this fleet are being found off Florida's coast even to this day. To provide a sense of scale to the enormity of this lost treasure, more than four tons of silver and gold have been reportedly retrieved from one wreck alone!

The thoughts of vast treasure apparently provided motive enough for Sam Bellamy to leave his wife and child half a world away. The lure of treasure allowed him to be successful in persuading a wealthy patron to finance a ship and crew to enable his adventure. After fitting out his newly acquired sloop with sufficient provisions and gear, he and his crew set of for the New World early in 1716.

British sloop circa 1716

According to folklore he came ashore at Eastham Harbor Cape Cod apparently to find rest and provisions before his continued trip south to Florida.

The Beginning of Bellamy's Pirating Career

By all accounts Sam Bellamy was a rouge and a simple, blustering windbag of a man. His adventuresome spirit and gift of gab had enabled him to finance his quest for gold and also to seduce the loveliest girl on Cape Cod, Goody Hallett.

From the Cape, Bellamy sailed to Newport, RI where he met Paulsgrave Williams. Paulsgrave came from a successful family. Bellamy was apparently successful in infecting Williams with gold fever and convinced Williams to contribute funds for his Caribbean adventure. The pair left Rhode Island together to begin their hunt for sunken Spanish treasure.

Whydah in a Storm

They searched for several months but, try as they would, had no luck finding any trace of sunken Spanish treasure as originally planned. Not wanting to return home as failures, together they decided that finding treasure on ships moving upon the surface of the water, rather than those sitting at the bottom of the sea, would be a much more profitable course of action. They would make their fortune as pirates.

Joined a "Pirate Training School"

The two men met the notorious pirate Benjamin Hornigold and decided to join his crew of cut throats. It would appear that Captain Hornigold ran sort of a pirate training school as it was upon his ship that the later infamous Blackbeard also first sailed the Caribbean as a novice pirate.

Captain Hornigold was born in England and accordingly would only attack French and Spanish ships, not English ships. In June 1716, his crew revolted against him because they wanted to attack an English ship.

The crew voted Samuel Bellamy and Paulsgrave Williams as the new Captain and Quartermaster, respectively.

Black Sam Bellamy

Bellamy and his crew plundered more than fifty ships making him one of the most successful pirates in the Caribbean. He was now known as "Black Bellamy" or "Black Sam". Perhaps his nickname, "Black", was a reference to his preference for the expensive black clothes he always wore. Dressed all in black, and with four dueling pistols around his waist, he was a formidable figure.

Black Sam was a fine strategist. He would employ two ships in his raids. The first, his flagship, was armed with many cannons but relatively slow. The second, captained by Paulsgrave Williams, was lightly armed but fast. With this combination of assets Black Sam was able to coordinated attacks and capture ships with relative ease without damaging them.

With his ship loaded with this treasure and the booty plundered from more than fifty other ships, Black

Bellamy and his crew decided to retire from pirating. They were now richer than their wildest imaginations could ever have imagined.

Black Sam and his crew set a Northerly course and headed for home. For some home was in New England; for others, home was further away in England. Where was Black Sam heading? Was he going home to the wife and child left in England, or was he returning, as promised, to the young farm girl he seduced on Cape Cod?

The Whydah sinks in storm off Cape Cod beach

Some, who believe he was returning for the Cape's Goody Hallett, will refer to Black Sam Bellamy as the "Romantic Pirate." If returning to Goody was his plan, perhaps those in England would call him a different name.

On April 26, near Cape Cod, Whydah and its crew of 148 souls ran into an intense late Winter storm. Despite Herculean efforts of the crew, the Whydah struck the bar off South Wellfleet near what is now Marconi Beach in the Cape Cod National Seashore Park and sank as raging surf tore her to pieces.

People along the beach watching the tragic scene reported hearing and seeing "Goody" Hallett high upon the dunes screaming thanks to the Devil for vengeance.

169

The next day a search for survivors and perhaps treasure revealed only bits and pieces of floating remains of the once proud flagship Whydah and her crew.

Paulgrave's ship, the "Mary Anne," had stopped at Block Island in Rhode Island so he could visit his mother and thereby avoided the storm.

Only two survived the Wydah's sinking and live to tell the stories of Captain Black Sam Bellamy: an Indian pilot and Thomas Davis, a Welsh carpenter. Nothing is known of what became of the pilot, but it was Davis' vivid account of the shipwreck that was passed from generation to generation to become part of Cape Cod folklore. Essentially all that is known of Black Sam the pirate comes from stories recounted by Thomas Davis. Thomas Davis was jailed, tried, and acquitted of piracy.

The Whydah's Bell

"The Encyclopedia Americana" says of Samuel Bellamy, "...a notorious pirate, was wrecked in his ship, the Whidah, of 23 guns and 130 men, off Wellfleet, on Cape Cod, in April 1717, after having captured several vessels on the coast and an indecisive engagement with a French ship proceeding to Quebec.

Only one Indian and one Englishman escaped of his crew. Six of the pirates, who had been run ashore when drunk a few days previous, by the captain of the captured vessel, were hung in Boston in November 1717. "Black Sam," as he was known by then, was never seen again, nor was his body ever recovered."

Was Captain Black Bellamy Tricked into Eternity?

In the spring of 1717, Bellamy and Williams are reported to have captured seven ships on their return trip to Cape Cod. Approaching the Cape, Consort Captain Williams, aboard sloop Mary Anne, stopped at Block Island, an island just south of Cape Cod, to visit family

The weather was deteriorating as the rest of Bellamy's fleet continued north to the Cape. One of the ships was a wine carrying sloop captained by a native Cape Codder. Legend has Bellamy promising this captain the return of his ship if he would lead the fleet into the safe harbor at Provincetown.

He was made this remarkable promise because he had extensive knowledge of the treacherous, shoaled waters off the Outer Cape known as the graveyard of the North Atlantic. The bones of literally thousands of hapless ships lay upon its sandy ocean bottom.

A lantern was hung in the rigging so that Bellamy and his flagship the Whydah would be able to follow in the darkness of the moonless night.

The wily Cape Cod captain apparently had other plans. He allowed the pirates left onboard to guard the prize to become drunk on the cargo of wine the ship carried. Then, with his captors thus incapacitated, he tossed a burning tar barrel overboard for the Whydah to follow into eternity via the sandy treacherous sandy shoals of the Outer Cape while he sailed safely into Provincetown harbor. Some of the pirates were caught in Provincetown, put on trial and hanged in Boston. Thoreau mentions the Whydah tragedy in his book, *Cape Cod.* He wrote,``A storm coming on, their whole fleet was wrecked, and more than a hundred dead bodies lay along the shore." The shore he references is Marconi Beach in Wellfleet.

171

I'm from the Government and I'm Here to Help

News of shipwrecked treasure traveled very fast. Within days officials in Boston sent a ship to the Cape to "protect the government's interests." In other words, confiscate the treasure.

Posters were immediately put up warning that anyone found with shipwreck goods would face a severe penalty. The government's men scoured the beaches, searched barns, sheds, yards and houses for miles around attempting to uncover booty of any kind. They confiscated several wagonloads of goods but no serious treasure was uncovered.

Prior to the arrival of the government ship, hundreds of men from all across the Cape had scoured the beach of anything of value. Reportedly the only thing left for the government team to recover was the pirate ship's anchor cable.

Centuries later the state of Massachusetts would claim joint ownership of the *Whydah* and demand to regulate the salvage of any artifacts and treasure it might contain. The difference this time was that lawyers were dispatched to confiscate treasure and not a ship.

After several years the suit was settled in favor of the treasure hunter Barry Clifford, the man who had invested fifteen years and countless dollars in order to find the treasure ship.

The Saga of Maria "Goody" Hallett – *Bellamy's Paramour*

It was here that young Sam Bellamy met and seduced the very beautiful Eastham farm girl, Maria Hallett, in the spring of 1716. Maria was a naïve fifteen year old farm girl from a well respected, church going Eastham family

The handsome sailor's sweet talk and tales of treasure and adventure impressed the wide-eyed Maria. He convinced her that he would marry her when he returned laden with silver, gold and jewels that he would recover from sunken treasure ships in the Caribbean. As Fall approached and the days shortened and grew cooler, he sailed south to begin his great adventure.

Goody Hallett

That Winter Maria was found lying in a cold Eastham barn with her dead baby in her arms. She was at once taken into town and attached to deacon Doane's whipping post and given several lashes before being thrown into jail. The selectmen spoke of charging her with murder. They said she must be made an example to others of the godless younger generation of the day.

It seemed that no cell could contain the young lass, and she continually escaped to wander the shore calling out the name of her lost love. Eastham gave up its attempts to keep her in jail and released the young girl upon the condition she would leave town and never return.

She made her home in a shack near the shore at South Wellfleet and eked out a living by doing menial jobs. In short order, the once most beautiful girl in Eastham had become haggard and worn and unrecognizable to those who had known her before Bellamy.

His Lover Labeled a Witch

Townspeople were convinced that she was a witch, and they now referred to as "Goody" Hallett. The name Goody, as defined in the American College Dictionary, was "a polite term applied to a woman in humble life."

Goody must have been extremely depressed and traumatized experiencing the death of her baby. Then to be shunned by friends and family, jailed then driven out of town combined perhaps causing her to lose her mind.

Witch on the Dunes

All of this happened in the era of the famous Salem witch trials so it was in keeping with the times for the town folks to condemn her as a witch, a person who had sold her soul to the devil. Goody would continually be seen walking the high Wellfleet cliffs gazing out to sea screaming curses into the winds on even the stormiest of Winter nights. Even today her ghost is said to walk the seaside cliffs of Cape Cod's outer shore near where Captain Black's ship went down in 1717.

Could witch Goody have had a hand in brewing storms that shipwrecked more than two thousand ships and drowned uncounted thousands of mariners, including her lover captain Black Bellamy, on the sandbars off South Wellfleet? There are those who believe she did.

On that fateful day in April 1717, at the height of the fierce storm, she was seen on the beach as the Whydah was sinking and sailors were drowning in the raging surf. People on the beach say they saw her high on the cliff shrieking thanks to the Devil for vengeance. All this happened off the South Wellfleet dunes near the lonely dilapidated shack in which Goody lived.

Goody Swallowed by a Whale?

"On April 22, 1751, she succumbed to the sea and was demolished by one of the whales off the coast. Further proof of this lies in the fact that when one of the whales was captured and cut open, inside they found Maria's red slippers."

Lynne McIlveen Illustration

Other tales have Goody riding upon the backs of whales with lanterns affixed to their tails in order to lure unsuspecting mariners onto the reefs and shoals of the outer cape referred to at the time as the "Graveyard of the Atlantic".

She is also supposed to have the power, as she was a witch, to conjure up storms and gales to the peril of seamen of the day. Some say it was she that brewed the storm that sank the Whydah and sent her scallywag lover to Davy Jones' locker.

Legend of "Goody's" Buried Treasure

Some legends say that "Goody" had retrieved a chest of pirate gold from the surf that stormy night and buried it somewhere in the Wellfleet dunes. Because "Goody" Hallett had "lost her mind" she apparently forgot where she buried the treasure for she continued to eek out a meager living until the day she died. If she did bury treasure, she kept the whereabouts a secret and took the location with her to her grave.

Treasure buried somewhere in the dunes

Another story of buried treasure has the two survivors Thomas Davis and John Julian visiting the house of Samuel Hardings in Wellfleet on the night of the disaster. According to the story...the next morning, the three men hitched up Hardings' wagon and retrieved several wagonloads of the wreck's treasure from the beach.

They secreted it in Hardings' barn before hiding it more securely, perhaps by burying the fortune somewhere on the Harding property.

About a week after the wreck, Governor Shute sent a Captain Cypian Southack to the Cape to recover as much of the pirate treasure as possible. He searched some private homes and commandeered some of the salvaged good but found no trace of the cargo.

Is there still buried gold somewhere in the Wellfleet dunes? Perhaps the treasure still lies beneath the sand where Goody buried it waiting to be uncovered or has it already been found?

It is rumored that Sam Bellamy's ghost still walks Wellfleet's cliffs and dunes in search of his lost treasure. To this day gold coins can be found on Wellfleet's beach after big storms.

The ghost of Black Sam Bellamy?

Treasure
in
Rhode
Island

Rhode Island, a Pirate's Haven

Piracy was a significant industry in Rhode Island and Newport a favorite refuge for pirates between voyages. Piracy was entrenched in Rhode Island from the mid 1600s through the early 1700s. In fact the other colonies would often refer to the state as "Rogues" Island.

A large number of pirates called Newport their home base. The problem the pirates presented was so severe that the London Board of Trade made an official complaint to the British government of the "great receptacle for pirates" at "Rode" Island.

In the 1690s, Newport was a major port in North America. Legal maritime activity was on the rise and increasingly rivaling piracy in economic importance. In 1695 and in response to the problem, the Earl of Bellomont financed an expedition by Captain Kidd against pirates "from New England, Rode Island, New York, and other parts in America".

Pirate Thomas Tew and New York's corrupt Governor conspire

The picture above is said to be of Rhode Island's notorious pirate Thomas Tew in conversation with New York's corrupt Governor Fletcher. Fletcher wrote in 1696 that "Rhode Island is now a free port for pirates. Thomas Tew brought there 100,000 pounds from the Red Sea in 1694."

In the 1720s under pressure from the British government, local officials decided they could no longer tolerate piracy. Legitimate commerce had overtaken piracy in economic importance and so the days of safe haven in Newport and environs came to an end. Many pirates were executed by hanging and buried on Goat Island in Newport Harbor.

Pirates, Privateers, & Smuggling

From 1650 until 1700, it could truly be said that piracy was an important industry in Rhode Island. Pirates fitted out in Rhode Island. Pirates obtained commissions in Rhode Island as a "privateer" that allowed them to capture the ships of an enemy, bring captured ships in Rhode Island and have the captured ship and contents legally declared property of the pirates (minus a percentage to the governor or government issuing the commission for someone to operate as a privateer).

A pirate bringing seized cargo ashore into Rhode Island was not paying custom taxes to England. To the English this was smuggling, avoiding payment of taxes. To the Rhode Islanders, this was simply part of everyday commerce, to pay pirates for goods at a cheaper price than otherwise available.

But cheaper goods was only part of a pirate's value to Rhode Island:

- For Rhode Island as a colony, getting a percentage "of the loot", was a government income without taxation of the local residents
- Privateering was a full employment policy for the colony: Rhode Islanders signed up as pirate crew members
- As a refuge and refitting base for pirates between voyages, Rhode Island was able to sell its own food, rum, lumber, goods, and shipbuilding repair services.

New Admiralty Court Established

Privateer Capt. John Hore was instrumental in Rhode Island establishing its own admiralty court -- outside of the Royal Admiralty Courts. In 1694, under a privateer's commission issued by English authority in Jamaica, Capt. Hore captured a fine French ship. He brought his prize back to Rhode Island -- instead of to New Providence in the Bahamas, because Rhode Island traditionally had not collected English customs taxes. Capt. Hore logically thought that by going to Rhode Island he would be able to avoid paying the English customs taxes, plus avoid paying the percentage due the British government in Jamaica.

However, upon arrival in Newport, Rhode Island Capt. Hore was dismayed to find there was at that time no Admiralty Court in Rhode Island to declare the property was legally his. Capt. Hore petitioned the governor of Rhode Island to establish an Admiralty Court. The governor complied declaring he thought it his patriotic duty, as an Englishman, to encourage attacks against the French, and Rhode Island quickly established an Admiralty Court. The newly established Court duly declared the captured French ship and her cargo legally that of Capt. Hore.

Capt. Hore settled in as a resident of Rhode Island for the winter, had the Rhode Island shipbuilders fit out his captured ship as a "privateer" and sailed off the next year to the Pacific's East Indies to be a pirate in that area.

Off to Rob, Pillage and Burn

"Privateer" Captain Colly was a Rhode Island pirate who brought in the *Pelican* a ship sized from the French. It was quickly refitted with 16 guns, and a crew of 100. Rhode Island Governor Walter Clares issued a customs clearance to have the *Pelican* sail to return a number of sailors captured on the *Pelican* to Jamaica.

Apparently many persons knew that Capt Colly and his crew intended "to cruise on the Moors, not intending to Pirate among the Europeans, but honestly and quietly to rob what Moors fell in their way."

Captain, Colly, promptly engaged and paid the Deputy Collector of Customs, Gardiner, to be his attorney and to take care of business for him while he was gone from Rhode Island, and Gardiner promptly cleared the ship for sailing from Rhode Island to Jamaica.

Capt Colly cruised off to Madagascar and is reported to have proceeded to do the "usual rob, pillage and burn" of settlements on islands near Madagascar.

Newport Justice

The trial of Pirate George Cutler illustrated how the legal system of Rhode Island was used as a refuge for pirates and to obtain the equivalent of what we today call "money laundering".

In 1698, Cutler was arrested for piracy and having a large sum of money in his possession which he had in his ship *Fowy*. He was immediately let out on bail, awaiting a trial. The rules of the trial were that if no one physically showed up to claim he was the owner of the cash and goods, the prisoner was acquitted and the court would declare the accused to be the rightful owner of the goods.

Cutler was tried before the Court of General Tryalls at Newport on the charge of piracy. No one offered any proof against him. Questioned where he had got the money, Cutler said it got it in various places, included being willed some of it by a resident of Madagascar. The jury acquitted; and Cutler took up residency in Newport, Rhode Island, with his stash of cash.

Usually, if a trial as to whether the accused was a pirate with stolen goods in his possession was not expected to clear the person accused of piracy, the prisoner took advantage of a wonderfully negligent succession of sheriffs and jailers. E.g., William Downs escaped from Jail in April 1698, it was duly reported that the Under Sheriff let Downs out of jail to "ease himself". No sheriff or undersheriff was ever tried for any crime or negligence.

183

Richest Piracy in History plotted at Newport's White Horse Tavern?

Was the White Horse Tavern the pirate's safe haven in Newport and where the plot to plunder the richest treasure of all time was hatched? Pirating by New England pirates was not restricted to America's east coast and the Caribbean; in fact New England pirates were to be found in every ocean and sea around the world. Birds of a feather flock together so, as one would expect, after returning to Newport the pirates would meet, perhaps at the White Horse Tavern, and swap tales of their adventures in far away waters. One can imagine pirate captains Joseph Farrell, William May and Thomas Tew swapping tales of their adventures, each attempting to better the stories of the other

Their tales would naturally progress to those of the richest "hunting ground" of the world. They would describe the unimaginable riches the richest persons on earth would transport across the seas once every year. The progression would lead these three men and two other pirate captains, William Want of Philadelphia and Captain Wake of Boston, to sail half way around the world into the Indian Ocean and the Red Sea in search of fantastic treasure.

White Horse Tavern

Once there they would meet up with the notorious pirate *Henry Every* and elect Every fleet captain and lead the capture of the largest treasure ship in history

The Target - The Great Moghul of India
Richest Man on Earth

Aurangzeb, aka Alamgir I (1618 – 1707). He was the
last of the great Mughal
emperors of India. He was
the son of Shah Jahan and
Mumtaz Mahal, for whom
the Taj Mahal was built.

Aurangzeb

He was Muslim monarch of
a mixed Hindu-Muslim
empire. He is reported to
have executed the Sikh
Guru Tegh Bahadur
thereby starting a Sikh-
Muslim feud that has
continued to the present.

He ruled India for 48 years
expanding the Mughal
Empire to its greatest
extent, encompassing all but the southern tip of the
Indian subcontinent. He remains one of the most
controversial figures in Indian history. His successors,
the 'Later Mughals', lacked his strong hand and the
Hindu Maratha Empire mostly replaced Mughal rule
during the rest of the 18th century.

The Pirate Fleet Assembles

In 1695, off Perim Island in the Red Sea, six pirate
ships assembled in preparation for raiding pilgrims
sailing from Mecca to India. The Newport pirates had
elected Captain "Long Ben" Every aboard his ship the
46 gun *Fancy* as fleet captain and they were itching to
plunder.

In the fleet was Thomas Tew, a native Rhode Islander
aboard his ship *Dolphin*. Tew had retired after
returning a rich man from his previous pirating tour

but apparently, the lure of additional riches and adventure were too much to resist.

Tew would sail to the Red Sea in consort with captains William Want from Philadelphia and his ship *Dolphin* and Thomas Wake of Boston on the *Susanna* reaching the Red Sea in June of 1695. Captain William May aboard the *Pearl* and the *Portsmouth Adventurer* captained by Joseph Farrell joined them there also.

This fleet of six well-armed pirate ships were now powerful enough to attack the heavily armored and protected treasure ships that plied the routes to and from Mecca. The pirates sighted two ships. The smaller of the two was the unarmed merchant ship *Fateh Mahmamadi*, carrying gold and silver valued at more than £50,000.

Pirate Ships sail to Red Sea

The second ship was the *Gang-i-Sawai*, one of the Great Moghul's largest ships bristling with an estimated eighty great guns and five hundred musketeers. Although outgunned the pirates did not hesitate to attack.

The Biggest Prize in History - Gold, Silver, Diamonds and 100 Virgins

Two lucky shots turned the tide in favor of the pirates. The first caused an explosion on the main deck killing the captain and the second dropped the mainmast hindering the ship's ability to manuever. In the ensuring two hour battle the now leaderless crew aboard their crippled ship finally surrendered to the pirates. The Gang-i-Sawai turned out to be the mother of all treasure ships.

Aboard the ship, the pirates would find treasure in gold, silver and diamonds estimated to be worth

Pirates do battle

$188,000,000 in 2,000 AD dollars. Each sailor's full share would be worth $3,500,000 today.

Boys under 18 would receive an amount in excess of a sailor of the day's lifetime earnings. According to all accounts, this was the greatest robbery of all time.

A daughter of the Great Moghul is reported to have been among the six hundred captured passengers that included more than one hundred beautiful virgins ages 12 to 18. They had been handpicked as additions to the Grand Mogul's harem. Captain Every claimed no harm befell the women. However, one pirate later confessed at his trial that the pirates committed "horrid barbarities."

When the Great Moghul learned of the attack, he vented his outrage on the English and the East India Company, threatening to force the English out of India. Assurances that the pirates would be brought to justice and heavy negotiations eventually calmed the Grand Moguls wrath.

Block Island

The Dutch first settled this island in 1661. It has been used by many pirates as a base for their movements between Spain, England and the New World. There are many rumors of buried treasures have been secreted on the island.

Block Island

In the old days Mohegan Bluff on Block Island was known as "Money Bluff" because of the huge treasure that everyone "knew" was buried there. Stories of the origins of that treasure are as varied and diverse as the variations of human imagi - nation.

One possible source is traced back to a group of French privateers that set up a base on the island in 1689, which they were later forced to abandon in a hurry leaving behind much of their plunder. Their treasure is said to be buried somewhere near "Money Bluff."

Sandy Point, on the northern end of Block Island, has been known to turn over old coins and relics here.

Two famous tales of treasure on Block Island.

The late author and treasure hunter, Thomas Penfield, wrote of two pirates, Captain Kidd and Joe Bradish, burying treasure on Block Island.

188

Captain Kidd

Kidd spotted two ships, the *"Fateh Mohammed"* and the *"Quedagh Merchant"*, both were sailing under a Flag of Convenience which in this case was French.

Kidd considered the ships legitimate targets for a Privateer sailing with the King of England's pass to attack the shipping of England' enemies and, as the king was at was with France, the two ships were fair game. He would later be hung for this action.

Captain William Kidd at the beginning and end of his career

The *"Quedagh Merchant"*, contained part of the enormous fortune, which was captured from the Grand Sultan of India returning from Mecca by the pirates Henry Long and Ben Avery. Also captured with the treasure was the Sultan's daughter.

Kidd sent a message to his old friend Lord Bellomont who was Governor of New York to arrange a safe passage for him and his crew. While waiting for Bellomonts answer Kidd landed some treasure Connecticut's Gardiners Island, He then stopped at Block Island before heading for Newport, Rhode Island.

Govenor Lord Bellomont had promised him safe passage but when Kidd landed he was arrested for

Piracy and sent back to England in chains Aboard HMS Advice.

He was in Newgate Prison awaiting trial, when he sent two essentially identical letters, one to the House of Lords and to the House of Parliament. The letters disclosed that he had treasure valued in the millions hidden on a particular island. His desire was to exchange this treasure for his freedom.

Unfortunately for Kidd the Molgul or Sultan of India

Grand Sultan

was incensed by the theft of his treasure by the English pirates and he was especially enraged by the kidnapping of his daughter.

The Mogul threatened to kick the English out of India, so Kidd's fate was sealed and he had to die to appease the Sultan. Kidd was found guilty, his letters ignored and he was hung at Tilbury Point on the Thames.

Back in America, Lord Bellomont had sent men far and wide searching for Kidd's Loot. Some chests were dug up from an orchard on Gardiners Island and returned to England where the contents were auctioned.

The proceeds from this auction were used to build Greenwich Hospital, which later became Greenwich Observatory, the irony of this is that Greenwich observatory is the Zero Datum point of Latitude for all shipping throughout the world today.

Locations in Rhode Island where Captain Kidd is reported to have buried treasure

Captain Kidd buried $40,000 in pirate gold on Patience Island in Newport County.

$60,000 in gold coins was secreted on the southerly tip of Hog Island by Capain Kidd at Pirates Cave. He left Thomas Paine behind to watch over his cache

Captain Bradish

According to Penfield, Bradish, who was part of Kidd's pirate crew, made a map of the location where Kidd's treasure was buried. He gave it to a companion before being taken to England and hanged.

However, this companion accompanied Bradish to

England to testify at the trial and never returned to America. Sources on Block Island maintain that there is a map leading to William Kidd's Block Island treasure as well.

Bradish, now captain of the *Adventure Galley,* brought aboard four sealed bags containing 2,805 pieces of eight and a bag of jewels. The *Adventure Galley* weighed anchor and sailed to Block Island, Rhode Island where the unloading the treasure began. Once the ship was emptied, the pirates fired guns into the bottom of the ship causing it to sink.

Gaspee Point

Located in Warwick, Rhode Island approximately seven miles south of Providence on the west side of Narragansett Bay. The beach in this area has been

Gaspee Point

turning up small artifacts and treasures from the wreck of the British schooner *Gaspee* since it ran aground here in 1772. It was then attacked and overcome by Patriots and set on fire.

The Prescott Farm

Located on route 114 in Portsmouth. Built in 1710, this farm was once owned by the Overings, one of the

Gold coins

wealthiest families in New England. The farm was also occupied by the British and General Richard Prescott. A rumor says that the General buried a large amount of gold coins somewhere on the farm just before the Patriots captured the farm in a raid.

Potterville Campsite

Located approximately one mile east of Potterville, on Town Farm Road. During the Revolutionary War, both the Patriots and the British used this area as their

Patriot campsite

camp. Often times, many relics, and small personal belongings can be found in these campsites. Buried caches have also been located. The reason being that the soldier wanted to protect his valuables in case of an attack. And at times, the soldier was killed, leaving the buried valuables behind.

Hope Island

In 1923 a fisherman located hundreds of gold and silver Spanish coins from the 1700's. More treasures may be lying in wait. Hope Island is located near the

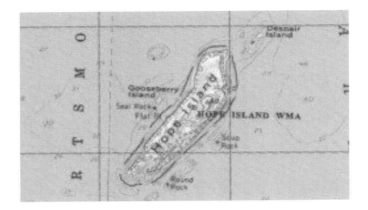

west side of Prudence Island in Narragansett Bay. Hope Island is a part of the Narragansett Bay National Estuarine Research Reserve

Newport

Up until the Revolutionary War, Newport was the fourth or fifth biggest city on the Atlantic seaboard and was a real center of commerce

The pirate Charles Harris, remarked just before he was hanged, that he had buried a chest of treasure on the beach at the base of Newport Cliffs. In 1949, a chest of treasure was located on the beach in that area. But before the individual who found it could get back with equipment to lift the chest, a tide came in and covered the large chest again.

Also, somewhere in Newport is a buried treasure worth $100,000 in 1700s dollars. It was buried by the pirate Thomas Tew.

Newport was also a major center of piracy during the late 17th and early 18th century. So many pirates used it as their base of operations that the London Board of Trade made an official complaint to the English government. Thomas Tew was the most famous pirate who made Newport his base, and he was very popular with the locals. After one of his pirating voyages, it was reported that almost the whole town came out to greet him.

Pirate Thomas Tew and the Govenor

In the 1720s, Colonial leaders arrested many pirates, acting under pressure from the British government. Many were hanged in Newport and were buried on Goat Island

Red Sea pirates sailed out of Newport Harbor, attacked Muslim ships, returned to Newport, sold plunder and spent foreign gold. Privateers who dabbled in piracy, pirates who pretended to be privateers and outright pirates all weighed anchor in Newport Harbor. Liars, thieves, murderers and rapists drank at local taverns and bribed their way to sanctuary.

Captain Kidd pursued Newport pirates until Muslim treasure drew him off course. Kidd sailed to Narragansett Bay to get help from Governor Cranston and Captain Thomas Paine. Captain Paine, retired Caribbean pirate, hid Kidd's treasure, helped found Trinity Church and led Rhode Island in her first naval victory.

Once Newport's prosperous shipping fleet was on the receiving end of piracy, its citizens turned dock lines into hangmen's nooses. Newport hung 26 Caribbean pirates in 1723; the largest mass execution in the colonies.

In the late eighteenth century another form of robbery threatened Rhode Island's shipping; taxation stole profits and British enforcement ships stole cargo. When colonists burned a British ship, the Gaspee, London called the perpetrators pirates and accused them of treason. Many of those perpetrators became privateers in the American Revolution.

Treasure in Connecticut

Great Windham Frog Fight
Windham

The story of the Great Windham Frog Fight was so bizarre it spread all the way to Europe during the 18th century. It was celebrated in song and print in the 19th century and commemorated by 11-foot frog sculptures in the 20th.

Here's the story: Tensions were running high in the frontier town of British colonists in the summer of 1754. The French and Indian War had broken out in May, and a drought threatened the crops of the farming community.

Shortly after midnight on a hot, muggy night in June, the residents of the town of Windham woke to a hideous sound, a shrieking, clattering roar.

Horrified, the townspeople jumped from their beds. Some thought the horrifying sounds were the war whoops of attacking Indians.

Lawyer Eliphalet Dyer – described by John Adams as 'longwinded' and 'tedious' but an 'honest, worthy man' -- led the town's militia in military readiness. The militiamen were said to have fired their muskets into the darkness throughout the night. By morning, the sound died down, and the townspeople celebrated their victory.

But as dawn broke, a scouting party ventured out toward the place from where the sound   . They realized the embarrassing truth. Hundreds of bullfrog corpses -- all belly up -- littered the landscape.

The sound had come from a pond belonging to Dyer. The drought had dried up all of Windham's standing water except for a puddle at the bottom of the pond.

A horde of frogs descended on that one remaining wet spot and fought over it.

What they had heard were the battle cries and dying moans of thirsty bullfrogs, magnified by the cloud cover and muggy air.

The story spread. At least three ballads were written about the Great Windham Frog Fight, and an 1888 operetta, *The Frogs of Old Windham*, was performed throughout Connecticut.

After the American Revolution, the Windham Bank issued banknotes with an image of a frog standing over the body of another frog.

The Windham Frog

The Willimantic section of Windham grew into a factory town that produced silk and cotton thread. The American Thread Company located on the banks of the Willimantic River and became Connecticut's largest employer.

Four 11-foot frogs sitting atop giant spools of thread guard today, the Thread City Crossing, or Frog Bridge.

The frog battlefield was renamed Frog Pond, which can be seen today a mile east of Windham Center on the Scotland Road. Look on the left as you cross Indian Hollow Brook.

Later, the town was burned to the ground during the French & Indian War. As was the custom of the day, residents, aware of an impending attack, buried their valuables. Many of the residents were killed leaving behind their caches. The old homes in town could be still hiding the colonist's valuables and await your finding them.

199

St. Mary's by the Sea

Bridgeport

St. Mary's by the Sea, a historic Bridgeport seaport of Black Rock, is a perfect site for finding jewelry and artifacts. Found here recently were two gorgeous rings. One ring was a rare opal. It was appraised at more than a $1,000 and the diamond ring appraised at more than $3,000.

There is a pile of rocks that can be viewed at dead low tide. These are the rubble ruins of a fort that defended

Black Rock Harbor through the Revolutionary War. In addition there is the stately Fayerweather Lighthouse across the harbor at the end of Seaside Park.

In the distance there is the haunted Penfield Reef Light where the ghost of Fred Jordan, a keeper who was taken by the Sound as he made his way across to the mainland for Christmas celebrations, now dwells.

In any event, this is a great place to enjoy being out in the fresh air.

Tales of Connecticut's shoreline hidden riches

Centuries after their last voyages, pirates still conjure elemental excitement in our collective imagination. We thrill to cinematic images of sleek sloops silhouetted by full moons sailing the Seven Seas in search of gold, silver, damask and jewels. Well into the 21st century,

legends and lore of famous pirates resonate along the shoreline and up the Connecticut River.

Tales of treasures yet unfound—and the supernatural beings that watch over them—are told and retold by those who love bygone days of adventure. Many folks hope to stumble across unimaginable riches buried on our shores by fearless corsair captains on long-ago moonless nights.

Pirate Treasures

Some A-list colonial American pirates may have buried treasure along the Connecticut coast and up the state's namesake river. Treasure hunters have found caches of gold doubloons. Other hoards of fabled riches still wait to be unearthed.

Charles Island off the coast of Milford suffered severe environmental damage due to gold seekers shoveling its sands. That town capitalizes on its buccaneering heritage with a yearly Captain Kidd Day festival geared toward family fun and economic development.

Thimble Islands
Skippers of tour boats that weave among the Thimble Islands spellbind their passengers with tales of Captain Kidd rowing ashore to bury loot on Money Island.

Money Point
There is also Money Point in Westbrook, where an eccentric professor spent years digging the beach at

low tide in hopes of turning up Kidd's gold. Would you be more successful using ancient dowsing equipment?

About Captain Kidd:
Captain William Kidd is one of the most enigmatic figures in buccaneer history. He exemplifies the larcenous, dashing (sometimes homicidal) sea rovers that sail through our reveries. He was a Scotsman anointed by New York's colonial governor and English nobility to lead a privateering voyage to, ironically, pursue pirates. He fell from grace when he captured a

treasure-laden vessel in the Red Sea that may or may not have been legitimate prey. This angered his supporters, who branded him a pirate.

On the island of Coromos, legend has it that he made the acquaintance of the Angel Moroni, keeper of the golden tablets that loom large in Mormon theology. The Angel purportedly taught Kidd how to summon ghosts and demons to do his bidding, and keep buried riches safe from gold seekers.

Upon his return to the New World, Kidd learned that he was an accused pirate with a price on his head. He sailed up the Atlantic seaboard and landed on Gardiner's Island in Long Island Sound.

Gardiner's Island

Kidd buried a portion of his ill-gotten riches on the island, where he lay at anchor in the summer of 1699.

Many small boats from Connecticut visited his ship. Some historians believe those boats returned home laden with gold, jewels, silver and fine cloth. Their comings and goings inspire the legends of demon guarded Kidd treasure that pique imaginations today.

The luckless captain then sailed to Boston to negotiate with the colonial governor. He was followed shortly by his Gardiner's Island treasure, but it was not enough to secure his freedom. Kidd was shipped across the Atlantic in chains and hanged on London Dock.

His body was encased in an iron cage and swung for years on the banks of the Thames River to warn seafarers away from the pirate life.

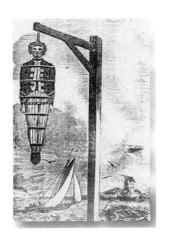

While the fabled buccaneer was burying his treasure on Gardiner's Island, another legend grew there. It involved the lord of the manor, John Lyon Gardiner purloining a large diamond and slipping it into a well bucket. James was a confirmed bachelor, but a resplendent beauty from Lyme named Sarah Griswold, out for a day sail, was blown onto his island by a gale. James was immediately smitten.

A few weeks later, he was rowed across Long Island Sound by 40 liveried oarsmen. He leapt ashore, muddying his kidskin boots, and presented a surprised Sarah with the nicked pirate diamond to pledge his troth. She said yes, and returned to Gardiner's Island as the bejeweled mistress of the manor, and James' bride. That, at least, is one version of the old story.

Lion's Rock

Lion's Rock in Old Lyme is one place where Kidd's treasure may repose. As the story goes, Kidd followed Moroni's instructions and installed a multi-headed demon fond of devouring humans to watch over his trove.

This horrible apparition can be thwarted, however, if someone reads the Bible while an accomplice digs up the booty. Modern day treasure hunters are frustrated because no one seems to know exactly where Lion's Rock is located. This elusive piece of granite is one site on the river that is believed to house Kidd's hoard.

Lord's Island, Haddam Island, Middle Haddam and Haddam Neck

These are all targets for metal detectors today. The Haddam Neck treasure was supposedly buried by two of Kidd's crewmen, and is guarded by the petulant ghost of the captain himself.

Wethersfield Cove

Farther upstream, Wethersfield Cove is another possible cache site. Generations of gold seekers claim

to have been frightened away from digging there by strange and terrifying noises and visions.

One would-be millionaire reported that he was chased by the ghost of William Moore—a sailor whom Captain Kidd killed by smashing his head with an oaken bucket for making mutinous remarks. To date, excavations in this area have turned up a few gold coins consistent with Kidd's time period.

Hopeful hunters can be seen scanning the brush surrounding the cove with metal detectors, trowels at the ready, should the pinging begin.

Clark's Island

Just across the Massachusetts line, Clark's Island is so entangled in treasure lore that most folks simply refer to it as Kidd's Island.

There are conflicting stories as to the nature of the shade that oversees that fabled cache of riches. Some say that after Kidd and several crewmen buried the booty, they drew straws to see who would remain on the island to keep watch over the loot. The bloke who came up short was promptly shot and buried beside the treasure chest. Kidd then used diabolical powers to ensure his specter kept the gold safe.

Guileless Maiden on the Earth

In a slightly more romantic version, the ghost of a

beautiful Creole girl, whom Kidd kidnapped from the Caribbean, watches over the island. According to some sources, she was interred along with the treasure so it could be, in Kidd's words, "watched over by the spirit of her who was once a guileless maiden on the earth."

Captain Kidd was not the only buccaneer to enlist spirits to safeguard Connecticut swag. In 1753, a Spanish Galleon, the San Jose y Helena, heavily laden with gold and silver, ran aground on a reef off New London. Badly damaged, she was towed to the town's docks. Her repairs, however, required the removal of her precious cargo so the ship could be careened. To no one's great surprise, most of it promptly disappeared. In a remarkably generous ruling, the General Assembly compensated the shipwrecked Iberians for their losses, and they happily sailed back to Spain.

Rumors and accusations as to who stole the treasure made their way around the Whaling City's taverns and taprooms, but no one was ever conclusively pegged as the perpetrator. Gradually, the town forgot about the incident and settled back to its seafaring ways.

Witch Granny Strickland

Some 70 years later, a convicted witch named Granny Strickland revived interest in the story. She had been banished from Connecticut for her necromantic activities and settled in Vermont, which had more liberal attitudes toward the Black Arts. She kept a set of clear rocks that she used as crystal balls in her arcane divinations. While in a trance, she claimed her magic pebbles revealed box upon box of silver coins and gold ingots.

They were buried, according to the numinous stones, under a dock in New London, and had lain there untouched for decades. The witch summoned her somewhat gullible grandsons, and enlisted them in her efforts to bring the bounty to the Green Mountain State.

With the boys, she sent a hand-drawn map that located the precious metals under a rickety, old unused wharf. In the small hours of the morning, the brothers made their way to the harbor's edge by lantern light and began to wield pick and shovel. Their hole kept filling with water and digging was difficult. Hot, tired and discouraged, the boys were about to abandon their quest when a shovel sparked against something hard: an ironbound chest. Granny's visions were validated. They dug as fast as they could until they gained a little purchase on the box and lifted it from its resting place. They wanted to get out of town before dawn. But beings from the Other World had different plans.

As they stooped to lift the heavy box, its iron bindings became white hot and impossible to hold. The air filled with deep growls and the vision of a giant dog filled their pit. Red eyes flashed around them in all directions, piercing the darkness. If that wasn't scary enough to dissuade them, a huge wild goose with blazing green eyes hovered above them, hissing horrible curses and spitting burning bile on the terrified treasure seekers. Granny had promised they would be safe, but these horrific haunts were too much for them. They dropped their tools and beat a hasty retreat out of New London. A disappointed Granny gave them some amulets and persuaded them to go back and try again, but the dock had disappeared.

The gold and silver from the Spanish ship were never found.

Salmon Brook

Not all Connecticut treasures are guarded by ghouls. In 1655, the pirate David Marteens captured a galleon with cargo worth an estimated $20 million. He was chased by other pirates and made his way up the Connecticut River to Windsor. The Puritans there wanted no part of pirates. But Marteens greased some

palms, and set up camp for a couple of weeks to repair his storm-damaged ship and bury his treasure. He made his way inland and dug a deep hole near what is now Salmon Brook. Lacking Kidd's mystical powers, he relied on stones marked with secret symbols to mark the spot where his money was interred. He sailed downriver to plunder some more and was never heard from again.

For a couple hundred years, treasure seekers would dig in the area in hopes of striking it rich, to no avail. But in the 1920s, a fellow named Nelson chanced upon some rocks inscribed with letters and numbers. He was unable to decipher them, so he enlisted the aid of a buddy named Ruches. Together, they found more stones but could not decyfer their hidden meanings.

Today, the treasure remains secure in sandy soil, awaiting someone with map dowsing skills.

These tales of demons may seem fantastical, but dreams of treasure and the age of pirates endure. The hulls of famous buccaneers parted Connecticut's waters. Their legacy and lore can be felt on foggy mornings when wisps of memory float along shoreline. We still stroll beaches in hopes of finding a doubloon

amidst the sea glass. The legends of these long ago looters are woven into the fabric of our imagination. Today's denizens of Long Island Sound and the Connecticut River celebrate the memories of famous freebooters, and keep their stories alive to thrill succeeding generations.

Other Books by Ted Burbank

- **A Guide to Plymouth's Famous Burial Hill**
  Includes an Index and map of headstone locations

- **The Golden Age of Piracy on Cape Cod and in New England** – *How New England became the pirate's headquarters, where treasure has and still might be found in New England*

- **Cape Cod Shipwrecks** - *"Graveyard of the Atlantic"*

- **Shipwrecks, Pirates and Treasure in Maine** –*America's first naval defeat, tales of shipwrecks, pirates and their treasure.*

- **Haunted Lighthouses of New England**
  plus haunted ships, forts, ghost ships and more

- **The "Islands" of Ocean Bluff and Brant Rock**
  Home of many American firsts

- **Put it Down! Go Out and Play**
  or *How to have fun without TV or Computers*

- ***A Homeowner's Complete Guide to Energy Independence***
  or How we eliminated our fuel and utility bills and attained "Zero Net Energy"

- **From the Garden of Eden to America**
  Chronicles Frank L Huddleston's ancestors journey from the Garden of Eden to Boston, MA

- **From the Garden of Eden to Plymouth Rock**
  Chronicles Theodore Parker Burbank and George Soule's ancestors journey from the Garden of Eden to Plymouth, MA

Any of these books can be ordered from Salty Pilgrim Press by going to www.SaltyPilgrim.com

Made in the USA
Middletown, DE
29 November 2020